DATE DUE

Fac. 92-3

FEB 21 1997

TWENTIETH-CENTURY INVENTORS

A M E R I C A N

P R O F I L E S

Twentieth-Century Inventors

■

Nathan Aaseng

Facts On File
New York • Oxford

Twentieth-Century Inventors

Facts On File, Inc.   Facts On File Limited
460 Park Avenue South   Collins Street
New York NY 10016   Oxford OX4 1XJ
USA   United Kingdom

Library of Congress Cataloging-in-Publication Data
Aaseng, Nathan.
    Twentieth-century inventors / Nathan Aaseng.
        p. cm. — (American profiles series : 2)
    Includes biographical references and index.
    Summary: Provides accounts of ten significant twentieth-century inventions and the people behind them, including the Wright brothers and their airplane, Robert Goddard and his rocket, and Gordon Gould and his laser
    ISBN 0-8160-2485-5
    1. Inventors—United States—Biography—Juvenile literature.
[1. Inventors.] I. Title. II. Title: 20th century inventors. III. Series.
T39.A37 1991
609.2'2—dc20
[B]
[92]   90-46547

A British CIP catalogue record for this book is available from the British Library.

Facts On File books are available at special discounts when purchased in bulk quantities for businesses, associations, institutions or sales promotions. Please contact our Special Sales Department in New York at 212/683-2244 (dial 800/322-8755 except in NY, AK, or HI) or in Oxford at 865/728399.

Text design by Ron Monteleone
Jacket design by Ron Monteleone
Composition by Facts On File, Inc.
Manufactured by The Maple-Vail Book Manufacturing Group
Printed in the United States of America

10 9 8 7 6 5 4 3 2

This book is printed on acid-free paper.

Contents

Introduction

The Wright Brothers, last of the celebrity inventors, demonstrate their latest airplane technology with this 1908 flight that lasted over an hour.

We have come full circle since the days of the first inventors. No one knows who first shaped a stone into a wheel as a means of transportation or discovered how to squeeze metal out of rock by applying fire. Generations of humans simply accepted the gifts of these nameless inventors and passed them on to their children.

Then came the age of the giants of invention. Tales were recorded of solitary individuals, often working with little but their hands and their own imaginations, who achieved stunning breakthroughs. Those who benefited from their genius could point to a product and put a name to the creator. Gutenberg and the printing press, Fulton and the steam boat, Whitney and the cotton gin, Morse and the telegraph, Bell and the telephone, Edison and the light bulb—virtually any schoolchild could recite the list.

But in the 20th century, inventors have returned to the ranks of the anonymous donor. Except for the Wright brothers, who closed out the age of the celebrity inventor, how many of the names in the table of contents are familiar? The average American would be hard-pressed to match one of these inventors with their invention. We take what they have given us without thanks or appreciation.

How is it that 20th-century inventors have fallen into the same obscurity as their prehistoric ancestors? Their inventions are at least as spectacular and far-reaching as those of any previous era. Thanks to the creation of such innovations as airplanes, plastics, computers, television, and lasers, technology has advanced more during the 20th century than in all previous centuries combined. Why are there so few household names among inventors anymore?

Part of the reason may be because they have been crowded away from the spotlight by more glittering personalities. We live in a society where trivia is elevated to an art form while those reponsible for some of the most sweeping changes in human history lie forgotten. Sports, entertainment, and society figures have far more eye-catching appeal than a very ordinary-looking person discussing the complex workings of a transistor.

Another explanation is that 20th-century inventors are buried under an avalanche of scientific data. Technology has advanced far beyond the ability of most people to comprehend it. We cannot actually see what a transistor or a cyclotron does; we can only see its effects. Overwhelmed by the instruction manuals and the technical explanations of how a refrigerator or computer or tape recorder works, we find it far easier simply to plug the machine in and not think about how it works. The stories of the inventors of these marvelous devices are thrown out along with the manuals.

There is something about scientific writing as well that destroys the appeal of modern inventors. Scientists take great pains to be completely objective in their work so as to eliminate human error. Their manner of communicating often leaves the public with the impression that great discoveries are made by white-coated humanoids instead of by real people who experience the same thrills and heartbreaks as the rest of us.

Finally, modern inventors have gotten lost in the bureaucracy of giant corporations. Many of the most earth-shaking inventions of recent times have been enormous enterprises. They have required the skills of a large team of experts and the financial backing of wealthy investors. When General Motors, Stanford University, or a joint venture of government and industry come up with a brilliant discovery, the credit must be split many ways. The heroes get lost in the sheer numbers of contributors.

Introduction

Yet even in the 20th century, innovations come, not from faceless corporations or from scientific robots—they come from individuals, real people with their own fascinating stories to tell. Who are the unknown heroes who have brought such drastic change to our world? What type of person is it who, without armies or fortune, is able to so dramatically alter the course of human events?

There are as many answers to this last question as there are inventors. Despite the common stereotype of the inventor as a superintelligent, absent-minded, eccentric, social misfit, the great inventors of the 20th century have been as different from each other as the range of human personality allows. Some were leaders; some were loners. Some were outspoken; some were quiet. Some craved recognition; some avoided it. Some came from prosperous, highly educated families; some had to scrap for everything they could get. Some had a keen eye for business; some enjoyed inventing just for the thrill of discovery.

There is really only one common bond that joins the inventors in this book. They all illustrate a point made by author Tom Peters, who has made a career out of analyzing excellence. Peters has observed that important changes in the world are almost always brought about by people who are driven by a powerful, single purpose in their lives.

The great inventors of the 20th century have not been 9-to-5 workers who watched the clock so that they could escape to their homes as soon as they had put in their expected hours. During their time of discovery, they were not what most people would call well-rounded individuals. They lived for their inventions at the expense of social lives, relaxation, health, and family concerns. Late at night, during weekends, in their spare time while working other jobs, they crammed as many hours of work as they could possibly fit into a day. Failures and obstacles only made them more determined to succeed. In every case it was as if the idea had taken over their lives and they could never be normal again until the thing was accomplished. Every invention of magnitude seems to demand a sacrifice of some kind on the part of the inventor.

This book focuses on the lives and achievements of American inventors. American inventors have had the advantage of working in an environment that fosters the creation of new ideas and products. The United States was scarcely in existence when Congress passed its first patent legislation in 1790. These laws rewarded innovation by granting exclusive manufacture and sales rights to the inventor of a product or process.

The patent laws have certainly done what they were intended to do. Since they were enacted, nearly five million patents have been awarded in the United States. Some of them have been for outlandish or frivolous inventions such as a coffin with an escape hatch. But also included among those five million are patents for some of the most important discoveries ever made, and an unusually large share of these have come from American inventors.

With their gifts and their dedication, 20th-century American inventors have broken through what we thought were the limits of our world. The limits of speed, power, access, material, and accuracy have all been stretched almost beyond imagination.

In breaking through the barriers of speed, 20th-century American inventors have accelerated the pace of life. The achievement of engine-driven air flight by the Wright brothers has accelerated the speed of transportation to the point where travelers can now

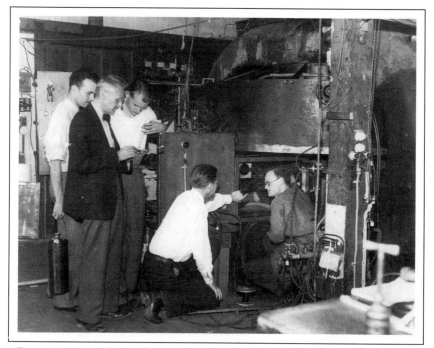

Ernest Lawrence (crouching in white shirt) and his assistants illustrate the growing reliance on group inventing efforts as he probes the interior of his 27-inch cyclotron. (Courtesy of Lawrence/Berkely Laboratory)

Introduction

go from New York to Los Angeles in a matter of hours. William Shockley's transistor has speeded up the rate at which our electric machines can perform work for us. Computers, pioneered by Howard Aiken, can now perform calculations in a matter of seconds that would take an unaided human hundreds of years to accomplish. The rapid rate of information exchange now available to us would not have been possible without Chester Carlson's dry-copy machine.

Inventors have uncovered vast sources of energy to power our world. Particle accelerators such as E.O. Lawrence's cyclotron have enabled us to tap into the almost limitless power of the atom. The laser, a product of Gordon Gould's imagination, has harnessed the searing and versatile power of light.

Twentieth-century inventors have given us access to sights, sounds, technical data, and space that were previously denied to us. Vladimir Zworykin developed a television that could allow our eyes to see thousands of miles away and into places too dangerous and too small for us to venture. The airplane freed humans from many of the limits of gravity. Robert Goddard's rocket innovations helped us break out of the remaining limits.

We now have material at our disposal that could not have been imagined in past centuries. Leo Baekeland's synthetic resin opened the door for countless structures and products that could not have been built from natural materials. The cyclotron helped manufacture artificial elements that have found a variety of medical, archaeological, and energy uses.

Finally, 20th-century American inventors have shattered the limits of accuracy and reliability in our machinery. Wilson Greatbatch developed a device so reliable that it can produce one beat per second in diseased hearts for up to 10 years without fail. Lasers can measure time and distance to the precision of dozens of decimal places. Computers can provide a level of mathematical accuracy far beyond the reach of the human mind.

It is often said of inventors that they were able to see more clearly because they stood on the shoulders of those who went before them. That is another way of saying that no one person can claim credit for the existence of the television, the laser, the computer, and so on. As was mentioned earlier, recognizing 20th-century inventors has been especially difficult due to the large numbers of people that have been in some way responsible for the final development of an invention.

In some chapters, this book focuses on those who stood on the shoulders of others. A great deal of electronics wilderness had to be cleared away by other inventors before Zworykin could get at the basics of the television camera and receiving set. Greatbatch could never have developed an implantable pacemaker without miniaturization. Gould and Shockley developed their ideas from knowledge acquired by other 20th-century scientists.

Other chapters profile those who provided the shoulders on which others stood. Aiken had little to do with developing the computer products we use today, but he provided a starting point from which the computer could grow. Goddard never was able to send a rocket into orbit, but he made it possible for those who came after him to do so. The impact of Lawrence's cyclotron was not so much in what the machine could do as in what others did with information provided by the machine.

In looking at the inventors and inventions of the 20th century, we are dealing with a moving target. Inventions and discoveries continue to be made at an astounding rate. The U.S. Patent and Trademark Office continues to be swamped with as many as 100,000 patent applications per year. Unlike the beginning of the century, when intelligent people declared that all important inventions had already been made, the possibilities for future inventions seem vast. Recently the U.S. Patent Office approved the patenting of life forms developed by genetic engineers. Not even the most adventurous scientist dares predict where that research will lead.

It may seem odd that a book about 20th-century inventors deals only with inventions conceived before 1960. But that is the result of the lag between when an idea takes shape and when it creates an impact on society. Even as we enjoy the novelty of the 20th century's technological wonders, people unknown to us are already working out the inventions that will alter society in the 21st century.

The Wright Brothers & the Airplane

Wilbur (left) and Orville Wright
(Library of Congress)

*I*n the fall of 1901, it appeared that the ancient quest for human flight had claimed yet another victim. Battered from several brutal crash landings in test flights, Wilbur Wright had to admit that his "new, improved" glider was a failure. Even more discouraging, the test results made no sense. The design had been based on careful calculations using the accepted data for such flight components as the amount of air pressure occurring at various wing angles. If Wilbur's suspicions were correct, much of the accepted data was worthless and anyone attempting to build an airplane would have to develop all the data from scratch.

1

That task seemed so enormous that Wilbur could see little point in continuing his pursuit of flight. Along with hundreds of professional and amateur tinkerers of the time, he was forced to admit that the problems were too difficult for him to solve. As he later admitted, "At this time I made the prediction that men would sometime fly, but that it would not be within our lifetime."

Two years later, Wilbur was gazing down at the sands of the North Carolina coast from his perch atop a flying machine. The machine had risen into the air on its own power and was actually flying into a stiff breeze! Unnoticed by the press and the public, Wilbur and his brother Orville had mastered a bewildering set of problems that had baffled so many brilliant inventors. In their spare time, with no financial backing except for the modest earnings from a bicycle shop, the Wright brothers ushered in a new era in transportation.

The Wright brothers' victory over gravity was forged in the fires of argument and debate. These exceptionally gifted young men were so bonded by the ties of family affection that they could survive long, stormy confrontations without any damage to their working relationship. Because of this, they were able to constantly challenge, examine, and improve upon each other's ideas. While these sessions were often so heated that observers were left aghast, the Wrights seldom let the passion of opinion mar their judgment. On at least one occasion, a furious debate ended with Orville being converted to Wilbur's opinion, and Wilbur to Orville's!

Wilbur was born on April 16, 1867, near Millville, Indiana; Orville was born August 19, 1871, in Dayton, Ohio. They were the third and fourth sons of an outspoken clergyman. Bishop Milton Wright's enthusiasm for his convictions led him to spend much of his life in a losing battle to influence the United Brethren of Christ to his way of thinking.

The bishop also held some strong and unusual ideas about education that helped shape his children's lives. He encouraged attention to detail by demanding long, very specific letters from his children during his frequent absences from home. His method of fostering independence was to advise the boys to take a day off from school now and then.

Milton also believed in the educational value of toys. In 1878 he gave Wilbur and Orville a toy helicopter powered by rubber bands.

The Wright Brothers

The curious Wright boys wore out the toy and then began building their own models. They were puzzled by the fact that the larger the model, the more difficult it was to fly. Neither of them, however, pursued the issue. There were other distractions for their inventive minds, such as inventing an automatic paper folder to help deliver newspapers published by their father.

Wilbur, an avid reader with a marvelous memory, was considered the brightest of the Wright children. But his future dimmed when he was smashed in the face by a hockey stick during his final year of high school. Although he recovered from injury, further complications involving his stomach and heart put the once-athletic Wilbur in very poor health. He was forced to abandon his goal of attending college and instead spent four years nursing his dying mother.

Orville, meanwhile, left high school without graduating and worked for two years as a printer's apprentice. The brothers had not been particularly close until Orville persuaded Wilbur to join him in producing their own newspaper in Dayton, in 1889. Their early efforts at cooperation proved difficult. They were not entirely trusting of each other and argued over how much work each was supposed to do. Instead of driving them apart, however, the arguments seemed to draw them together. They enjoyed matching wits with each other because they were both quite skilled at debate.

Neither Wilbur nor Orville ever married. For Wilbur it was apparently a matter of being too engrossed in his work to bother with a social life, whereas Orville was painfully shy. Orville was closely attached to his siblings and throughout his life was even closer to his younger sister, Katharine, than he was to Wilbur. When Katharine married later in life, Orville considered it an act of disloyalty and refused to speak to her for years.

When their printing venture failed, Wilbur and Orville drifted into a new vocation. Bicycles had become the rage in the early 1890s and, with their love of machines, it was not surprising that the Wright boys took up biking as a hobby. Word spread among their friends that the Wrights were experts at repairing bikes. Before long, Orville and Wilbur were in great demand. By autumn of 1892, they had received so many requests for bicycle maintenance that they opened a bicycle repair shop. Gradually, they branched out into building and selling their own models of bicycles.

Twentieth-Century Inventors

The Wright Cycle Company was going well when, in 1896, the spectacular death of Otto Lilienthal caught Wilbur's attention. Lilienthal, a German, had performed nearly 2,000 courageous experiments with gliders before plunging to his death in an accident. Wilbur's old fascination with the toy helicopter rekindled, and he began reading on the subject of human flight. But it was not until 1899 that he was spurred into action. At that time he read a book on ornithology (the study of birds) and became, in his own words, "afflicted with the belief that flight is possible to man." As with the other inventors in this book, once his interest had been aroused, it would be appeased only by a successful invention.

Wilbur's "disease," as he referred to it, was merely one case in a widespread epidemic. Following the development of the internal combustion automobile in the latter 19th century, a great many people were eager to try the next step in the evolution of transportation: machine-powered flight. President William McKinley's administration, heading into a war with Spain, was so intrigued by the military possibilities of an airplane that it granted $50,000 to a leading scientist, Samuel Langley, to develop such a vehicle. The lure of a $100,000 prize offered by promoters of the 1904 World's Fair in St. Louis coaxed many other inventors to attempt the dream that had baffled humans since the ancient stories of Icarus—who, according to Greek myth, flew to his death on wings of feathers and wax. From the laboratories of famous men such as Thomas Edison and Alexander Graham Bell to the garages of rank amateurs, inventors throughout the world raced to become the first to fly.

When Wilbur Wright contacted the Smithsonian Institution for information on aviation, however, no one had come close to flying. There had been nothing but a few brief air hops in some European countries. Many government officials and aviation experts were growing tired of hearing about all the hare-brained schemes and colossal failures.

The Smithsonian's response to Wilbur mentioned the name of aviation historian and engineer Octave Chanute. The letter that Wilbur then wrote to Chanute might easily have been ignored among the sea of letters that the expert received from airplane enthusiasts. But the historian was impressed with Wilbur's grasp of aeronautic principles. Instead of trying to impress people with some brilliant scheme, Wright simply expressed a desire for further information. Chanute struck up a correspondence with

4

Wilbur and directed him to information on the subject of aeronautics.

One of Wilbur's greatest gifts was the ability to separate useful facts from a mound of complex statistics. He quickly determined that the science of air flight consisted mainly of guesses with little solid evidence to back them up. As Wilbur saw it, the problem of powered, heavier-than-air flight could be divided into three components: a suitable wing structure to produce the upward lift, an engine to produce the forward motion, and a means of controlling the structure while it was in flight. It seemed to him that the first two problems were very nearly solved. Gliders had been built that could carry humans in flight, and automobile engines had been built that could provide necessary thrust. The key to designing a workable airplane, then, was to develop control. Previous efforts had relied on little more than shifting the body weight from one side to the other to maintain balance, and Wilbur saw that this was not enough.

Wilbur was a quiet man who often withdrew into his own world when a problem of particular interest arose. While puzzling over the problem of control, he observed birds in flight and saw how they balanced themselves by twisting their wing tips. Perhaps that was the secret to controlling an airplane. Alone in the bike shop one day, he was holding an empty inner tube box when it suddenly occurred to him how he could simulate this wing-twisting on a human-made glider. By twisting one side of the flimsy box one way and twisting the other side in the opposite way, he could achieve the desired wing twist. He then showed Orville his plan to *warp* the wings, that is, to curve the forward edge of one wing downward while curving the trailing edge of the other down.

Wilbur built a model with a five-foot wingspan and attached cords by which he could control the wing-warping. In July 1899, he flew the model and found that his system worked well. He then set about building a full-sized, human-supporting glider with which he could further test his ideas about wing structure. Along with the cloth wings and warping cables, he added an *elevator*, a small surface at the front of the plane to provide extra lift and stability. Business at the bike shop generally began to dwindle beginning in September, and so he chose to devote that time of year to experimenting with his model, which he would fly as a kite on the end of a rope.

Wilbur did not like to leave anything to chance. He examined reports from the United States Weather Bureau to find a suitable place for kite flying. Kitty Hawk, North Carolina, along the Atlantic Coast, was rated the sixth windiest location on the charts, and it offered the advantages of a sandy, treeless landing area and isolation from curiosity seekers. After making careful calculations, the kite was built, and Wilbur traveled to Kitty Hawk in September 1900.

Orville was gradually drawn into his brother's fascination with flying. A meticulous, neat person, Orville had a knack for contributing creative solutions to mechanical problems. While Wilbur was setting up his experiments in Kitty Hawk, Orville decided that he, too, could get away from the shop for awhile and he joined his brother.

At first, Wilbur attempted to launch himself from a tower and fly at the end of the rope along with the kite. But on his first try, he felt a loss of control and quickly shouted to be pulled down. Mindful of the example of Lilienthal and others, he was not about to sacrifice his life in the name of science. Despite his painstaking calculations, something was not working quite right. The Wrights decided to conduct most of their experiments with a pilotless glider-kite. They flew their warped wing model in a variety of winds, carrying different weights, and recorded such data as *air resistance*, the degree to which a moving object is slowed down by the air through which it travels.

But Wilbur did not want to return to Dayton without at least trying to glide. After determining that he would have best results lying on his stomach, Wilbur had Orville and another helper launch him into some short glides down gentle, sandy slopes. The success of these brief glides fueled the Wrights' enthusiasm for continuing their efforts, despite their confusion over the contradictory results of their experiments.

The next fall, the Wright brothers returned to Kitty Hawk with a much larger glider, one with a wingspan of 22 feet. Their calculations of the optimum wing shape, based on air pressure tables compiled by Lilienthal and others, led them to put more *camber*, or lengthwise bend, in the wings. This new design, they hoped, would make it possible for them to fly even when there was relatively little wind.

These gliders would be piloted, with the pilot lying in a movable platform called a cradle in the center of the glider. When one wing dipped, the pilot merely shifted his weight, pulling the cradle to the other side. As the cradle moved, wires attached to it would warp the wings into the proper shape, or configuration.

The Wright brothers perform repairs on one of their early models.

This time they attempted more than 100 flights in their glider. But to their frustration, the glider performed poorly, worse than their glider of the year before. The Wrights had come to suspect that the existing data on wing angles and air pressure was wrong.

Having lost confidence in the data on which they based their calculations, the Wrights saw little point in continuing their flight experiments. But, encouraged by Chanute, they finally set up a homemade experiment to test the accuracy of the accepted tables. They mounted a bicycle wheel in a horizontal position on another bicycle. Two simulated wings were attached to the wheel in specific areas, one of them with a cambered surface and one with a flat surface. According to the accepted data, the lift provided by those two surfaces should counteract each other, so that the wheel would not spin.

The Wrights pedaled their experimental bike down the street and found that the wheel did turn—the tables were wrong. They then set up their own wind tunnel in their bike shop so they could find out the correct measurements for themselves. This wind tunnel consisted of a 6-foot-long wooden box with an opening of 15 square inches. At one end of this box they attached a fan. At the other end, they inserted the test materials. They tested over 200 types of wing surfaces and obtained data that was remarkably accurate for a homemade device.

By this time, the quality of their experiments was becoming recognized, and they received offers of financial aid. The Wright brothers, however, refused them all. This was their project, and they were going to do everything their way. They wanted no help or interference from anyone.

Based on their new, accurate tables, the Wrights constructed a glider with longer and thinner wings than their old ones. The camber was reduced, and the wing was constructed so that its highest point was one quarter the distance from the wing's front edge. A fixed rudder was added to correct the problem of increased air resistance, or drag, that occurred when the wing tips were warped. A movable elevator was installed in the front of the plane. By adjusting the angle of this elevator the plane could climb or dive, or be prevented from doing either.

The Wrights' tests in 1902 showed that they were on track—in fact, far ahead of anyone else in the field. Despite the improvement, though, the glider was still difficult to control, especially in sharp turns. After a frightening crash in a September trial, Orville suggested replacing the fixed rear rudder with a hinged one. The problem was, he believed, that whenever a wing dipped it increased the drag on that side of the plane. This increased drag could be offset by turning the surface of the rudder to supply more lift. The same cables that connected the cradle to the wing tips could be modified to include control of the rudder.

With this addition, the Wrights' #3 glider floated smoothly down the Kill Devil Hills outside Kitty Hawk in October 1902. Orville joined Wilbur in learning how to operate the control system. Between the two of them, they sailed on more than 1,000 controlled glides into winds gusting up to 35 miles per hour. The longest of these touched down 622½ feet from the takeoff point on a flight lasting 26 seconds.

Within a year of conceding that the task was hopeless, the Wrights had mastered the problem of midair control. After returning home, they applied for a patent for a control system that included coordination of the wing warp to control lateral, or side-to-side rolling, an elevator to keep the plane from drastically rising or plunging, and a movable rudder to control turns. The problem of flight, they were certain, was solved. All they needed to do was add an engine to propel the craft.

With his usual thoroughness, Wilbur calculated that their plane could carry a load of up to 625 pounds. Allowing 140 pounds for his own weight, and 285 pounds for the frame, that left 200 pounds for all the mechanical equipment. Wilbur wrote to various automobile manufacturers asking if he could purchase a 12 horsepower engine weighing 160 pounds. When this inquiry brought no response, the Wrights built their own engine, with the help of a friend, Charlie Taylor.

Meanwhile, Wilbur investigated books on marine engineering for information on how to adapt the engine to air travel. It was obvious that in order for an airplane to sustain flight, it would have to churn through the air much as a boat churned through water. Unfortunately he was again disappointed by the lack of reliable research. It was left to the Wright brothers to argue, shout, and reason their way past all remaining obstacles. Eventually they settled on a two-propeller design. In order to keep the spin of the propellers from veering the plane to the right or left, they had the props spin in opposite directions.

The finished airplane weighed in at more than the desired 625 pounds, but this was balanced by output from the Wrights' engine above that estimated in the earlier weight calculation. *The Wright Flyer*, named after one of their bicycle models, was ready for testing in the fall of 1903.

But their competitors in the race to be first in flight had not been idle. While the Wrights' plans were delayed by engine malfunctions and damaged propeller shafts, Samuel Langley was preparing to edge them out of a place in history. After seven years of secretive, government-backed research, he declared that his manned "aeroplane" was ready for public demonstration. On October 7, 1903, Langley's contraption roared down a launching system that was built onto a houseboat. The plane sailed off the launching rail and fell straight into the Potomac River, "like a handful of mortar," according to one witness.

Believing the failure to be a result of a faulty takeoff, Langley tried again on December 8. This time the pilot nearly drowned when the craft plunged into the icy river.

A few days later, on December 14, the Wrights were finally ready for their trial run. Wilbur won the coin toss and thus the right to make the world's first manned, heavier-than-air, engine-powered flight. While he lay prone in the cradle of the plane, assistants

Wilbur watches as Orville lifts off from the launching track on December 17, 1903, in the first successful airplane flight.

pushed his craft down the slope of the 60-foot launching track. The plane, with its 40-foot wingspan, rose into the air. But almost immediately the nose turned up sharply, and the plane crashed on its left wing.

The Wrights decided that the downhill run had caused the plane to build up too much speed. After repairing the damage, they set up their single-rail track on a flat section of ground. Not only would this reduce the takeoff speed, but it would provide better evidence that the plane was moving under its own power.

Blustery winds delayed the attempt until December 17. Then, although cold winds continued to blow at 27 miles per hour, the Wrights decided they could wait no longer if they wanted to make it home for Christmas. It was Orville's turn to pilot the experiment. The balky engine was started and the machine started down the track. Wilbur had positioned a photographer at the end of the rail to record the moment of success. The plane lifted into the air and wobbled into the stiff breeze for 12 seconds, covering a distance of 120 feet and landing smoothly on its sledlike skids. Three flights later, Wilbur guided the craft on a 59-second flight and touched down in the sand 852 feet from the starting point. The Wrights were confident of an even longer flight, but a gust of wind blew the plane over and damaged it too much to continue.

Oddly, only a few scattered newspapers carried the story of the Wright brothers' historic flight at Kitty Hawk. The endless procession of cranks with their phony flying machines had soured the press on the subject of airplanes, and most refused to credit the story. Even though the Wrights flew more than 120 times in the next two years over a friend's pasture near Dayton, many doubted that they had ever gotten off the ground. The United States Army ignored Wilbur's offer to build a plane for them.

Fearful of their designs being copied, the Wrights offered no public proof of their claim to be first. Other aviators managed to stay aloft for increasing periods of time, and there was great debate over who was the first to fly. In 1908, Wilbur finally demonstrated for a French audience that the Wright brothers were far ahead of any other pioneer aviators. They could fly for more than two hours and bank into turns with astounding grace and agility.

The Wright brothers formed an airplane manufacturing company in 1909 to take advantage of their patents. But the brothers' involvement with aviation ended with Wilbur's sudden death from typhoid fever on May 30, 1912. Without his lifelong partner and the driving force behind their experiments, Orville lost interest and sold all of his shares in their thriving Wright Aeronautical Company. Although he continued to perform airplane experiments, he had nothing more to do with airplane manufacturing and he made no further lasting contributions to the field.

But by the time of Wilbur's death, other aviators were streaming through the doors that the Wrights had opened. In 1909, the English Channel was crossed by airplane. In 1911, Cal Rodgers completed a flight across the United States, and Italian planes were flying military scouting missions in North Africa. A year later, Bulgarian pilots dropped bombs from their aerial perches.

Within 12 years of that first wobbly flight, humans were soaring as high as 5,000 feet into the air, at speeds of up to 125 miles per hour. A German plane had stayed in the air for 24 continuous hours, and a Russian model had carried 16 passengers on a flight.

By the time of Orville's death on January 30, 1948, the development of the airplane had shrunk the world considerably. Trips that had once taken days and even weeks could be accomplished in a matter of hours. During the 1980s, major passenger carriers in the United States were making over five million takeoffs per year. They were flying more than three billion miles per year, the equivalent of 40,000 trips around the world. Airplanes have so shrunk the distance between cities that a United States SR-71 jet has covered the distance from Southern California to Washington, D.C., in just over an hour.

The ability of people to travel through the air at great speeds has produced profound changes in many areas of life, from international commerce, tourism, and mail delivery to diplomacy and warfare.

As with many inventions, some sort of airplane would probably have been invented eventually without the Wright brothers. Wilbur deflected claims that he was a genius by declaring that more luck than skill was involved: "If the wheels of time were turned back, it is not at all probable that we would do again what we have done."

But it was the Wrights, with chief credit going to Wilbur, who piloted in the age of flight. The method of flight control that they developed remains the basis of all fixed-wing air transportation today, a lasting tribute to the genius of the bicycle mechanics from Dayton, Ohio.

Chronology

April 16, 1887	Wilbur born near Millville, Indiana
August 19, 1871	Orville born in Dayton, Ohio
1878	boys receive rubber band–powered helicopter as a gift
1889	Wilbur and Orville work together to publish a newspaper
1892	they open bicycle repair shop
1899	Wilbur develops interest in aviation and begins inquiries on flight
1900	Wrights begin first test flights at Kitty Hawk, N.C.
December 17, 1903	Orville pilots the first manned, heavier-than-air, engine-powered aircraft flight
1904–05	Wrights' airplane design perfected in tests near Dayton
1908	they perform public demonstrations, proving their expertise
1909	Wilbur and Orville form Wright Aeronautical Company, an airplane manufacturer
May 30, 1912	Wilbur dies at age 45
January 30, 1948	Orville dies at age 76

Further Reading

Crouch, Tom. *The Bishop's Boys*. New York: W.W. Norton, 1989. Written by an aviation historian, this book provides a detailed and thoroughly documented look at the Wright brothers. Although not overly complex, its length (more than 500 pages) may be intimidating.

Franchere, Ruth. *The Wright Brothers*. New York: Harper & Row Junior Books Group, 1972. An illustrated volume written for young adults focusing on the lives and achievements of the Wright brothers.

Reynolds, Quentin. *The Wright Brothers*. New York: Random House, 1981. An account of the lives of this famous pair designed for young readers.

Sabin, Louis. *Wilbur & Orville Wright: The Flight To Adventure*. Mahwah, N.J.: Troll Associates, 1983. A brief (48 pages) account of how the Wrights invented the airplane. This book pays more attention to the technology and the invention itself than to the lives of the inventors.

Sobol, Donald J. *The Wright Brothers at Kitty Hawk*. New York: Scholastic, 1987. Designed for young readers, this illustrated book tells the story of the Wright brothers and their accomplishments.

Wright, Orville. *How We Invented the Airplane*. New York: McKay, 1953. Orvill's memoirs provide an inside view of the Wright brothers' triumph. Historians note, however, that Orville tends to exaggerate his own contributions compared to his older brother's.

Leo Baekeland & Plastic

Leo Hendrik Baekeland
(Library of Congress)

*F*or most of human existence, nature has been the sole supplier of raw materials for construction of items we need and enjoy. Nature's inventory included plant products (such as wood and cotton), animal products (such as leather and bone), and materials from the ground (such as metal and stone). Although this variety of materials was ample for most occasions, there were times when none of the available materials quite fit the need. In those cases, people simply had to make do with what they had and accept the results.

Leo Hendrik Baekeland started the stampede that changed all that when he created a brand new substance. In 1909, by carefully controlling a reaction between two common natural compounds, Baekeland came up with a new material that did not occur in nature. In many ways, his invention was superior to anything nature had to offer. His Bakelite was strong, yet lighter than stone. It did not rust or conduct electricity, like metal. Unlike wood, it could be molded into any desired shape. Yet it was cheaper to produce than any of the natural materials.

Suddenly chemists all over the world began combining chemical substances similar to those used by Baekeland to see what kinds of materials they could produce. Within 35 years of Baekeland's first completely synthetic material, more than 5,000 human-made substances had been developed. These materials became known as plastics, and they have provided the world with building blocks for entire new industries. Plastics have so overwhelmed the world that, 75 years after Baekeland's breakthrough, it is often considered a special feature if a product is *not* made out of plastic.

Leo Hendrik Baekeland was born in Ghent, Belgium, on November 14, 1863. The paths that Baekeland took in finding a career in chemistry were not paved by any family traditions or influences. Neither his father, who worked as a shoe repairman, nor his mother, who worked as a maid, could read or write.

In any event, Leo was not the kind of boy to let others direct his interests. When he took on a hobby, he did so with such gusto that the hobby became the cornerstone of his life. For many years, young Leo's dream was to run away to sea. In preparation for this wonderful adventure, he quickly mastered the subject of geography, while spending only enough effort in his other subjects to get by.

Eventually he found a hobby even more exciting than the sea, and that was what led him into his chosen career. The new hobby was photography. Again, Baekeland sacrificed schoolwork for the sake of his passion. On many nights when he was supposed to be studying in his room, he secretly pulled out his equipment to develop photographs he had taken during the day.

But he quickly discovered that in order to accomplish much in the field of photography, he needed to learn about the chemicals involved in the process. Because his school did not teach any subjects that had to do with photography, young Baekeland had to turn to night school at the Municipal Technical School of Ghent to satisfy his curiosity. When Baekeland put his mind to one of his pet subjects, the result could be astounding. His teachers at the Municipal Technical School were amazed at how quickly he caught on to the concepts of chemistry.

Baekeland was only too eager to try out some of his newly acquired knowledge on his own. Once he found himself in desperate need of silver nitrate solution to develop some film. With no money to purchase new supplies, the youngster made use of his chemical skills to extract the needed silver from a watch that a relative had given him. After dissolving the silver watch chain in nitric acid, Baekeland figured out a way to separate the impurities so that he could obtain a high-quality solution of silver nitrate.

Baekeland showed such promise in chemistry that he was admitted as a full-time student to the University of Ghent at the age of 17. Within four years, he earned his doctorate degree in chemistry. After serving as a lecture assistant, he accepted a job as a professor of chemistry and physics at the Government Normal School of Science in Bruges in 1887. He won first prize in a chemistry contest for graduates of Belgian universities, and, in 1889, the 26-year-old Baekeland was offered a post as assistant professor of chemistry at the prestigious University of Ghent. Baekeland seemed firmly entrenched in the world of academics, an appearance that was reinforced by his marriage to Celine Swarts, the daughter of one of his former chemistry professors.

But Baekeland, who still loved to chase after his own interests, found the routine work at the university to be confining. He was pleased when, as one of the rewards for his academic excellence, he was granted a three-year fellowship to travel abroad to learn new methods and insights in the chemistry of photography. It was a perfect combination of interests. At last he would be fulfilling his old dream of taking to the sea, while at the same time pursuing his main love—photography! After visiting England and Scotland, the Baekelands sailed to the United States, where such pioneers as George Eastman were making giant strides in simplifying the art of taking and developing pictures.

While in New York, he spoke with some businessmen who were so enthusiastic about the photography industry that Baekeland could not resist an offer they made to him. He accepted a job from the E. & H.T. Anthony Company, a leading manufacturer of photographic paper, cabled his resignation to the University of Ghent, and settled into life in a new country.

After two years of work, the independent-minded Baekeland set off on his own and opened his own consulting laboratory in New

York City. With his new-found freedom, Baekeland hardly knew where to focus his energy. "I tried to work out several inventions, the development of which would cost a fortune in subsidies," he later said. In poor health, with no money and mounting debts, he came to the sober conclusion that he was wasting his time on grandiose dreams far beyond his budget. He decided to focus on one simple project at a time, beginning with a new method of extracting tin from ore. An explosion and a near- tragic laboratory accident scared him away from completing that project. With little to show for his independent efforts, Baekeland retreated to the safety of his primary area of expertise—photography.

One of the main nuisances of photography at the time was that prints of pictures could only be made when the weather cooperated. There was no way to get a clear print unless the sun was shining. In 1893, Baekeland broke through that restriction with the development of a colloidal silver nitrate paper that he called Velox. This paper was sensitive enough that pictures could be printed under less intense, artificial light (at this time, gaslight).

To take advantage of his invention, Baekeland started a new company in partnership with businessman Leonard Jacobi. The Nepera Chemical Company, as the venture was called, faced a discouraging array of problems. The business was founded just as the United States economy was falling into a depression. Professional photographers, who had grown accustomed to printing in sunlight, were suspicious of this shortcut method. In fact, one of those who did try it wrote to Baekeland that "your paper is the greatest photography swindle of the age." (It later turned out that the photographer had failed to follow directions.) Further, heat and humidity could cause problems in the production of his paper. In an age before air conditioning, Baekeland had to design his own system of controlling the climate of his production facilities.

Baekeland was fortunate during this period of stress that he had the continued support of his wife, whom he once said deserved a great measure of credit for his success. For it was only after Baekeland spent "several years of hard work, with never a single day of rest, and ever wondering if I would pull through or not," that he gained the trust of amateur photographers. Velox gaslight photography paper proved so reliable and easy to use that it attracted the interest of George Eastman of the prosperous Eastman-Kodak Company. In 1899, Baekeland was invited to visit Rochester, New York, to discuss selling his process to Eastman.

Leo Baekeland & Plastic

While riding the train to Rochester, Baekeland put a value of $25,000 on his invention. Fortunately for him, Eastman opened their negotiations with an offer of somewhere around $1 million!

Baekeland eagerly sold out. At the age of 36, he and his family were financially set for life. But instead of coasting on his success, he became ever more fascinated with the possibilities of chemistry. With the money from the sale of Velox, he equipped a new laboratory at his estate in Yonkers, New York, where he was free to work on whatever he pleased without worrying about whether or not he could pay the bills.

After dabbling in electrochemistry for awhile and returning to Europe for a period of study, Baekeland was struck by a new passion in his life. Beginning in 1902, he experimented with two types of simple chemicals knows as phenols and aldehydes. By 1905, these experiments became as much of an obsession as his old photography hobby. Baekeland was intrigued by the possibility of discovering a valuable artificial substance from the combination of common chemicals.

Baekeland was not the first person to try such a thing. In 1856, a London student named William Henry Renkin had accidentally created a deep purple dye from a chemical experiment performed on a residue of coal tar. A number of commercial uses were found for this dye, and it was sold profitably.

This alerted chemists that there was a great deal of money and fame to be gained from creating new substances, such as dye, from inexpensive *organic* materials. Organic chemicals are simply those that contain carbon. Carbon atoms are able to link up easily with other atoms to form a wide variety of molecules. Carbon can combine with a few atoms to form simple molecules such as methanol. It can link into long, complex chains of molecules to form substances such as waxes and proteins. Chemists had discovered that many of the natural products that humans used, such as cotton, wool, and silk, were actually products formed from even more basic carbon materials.

Following Renkin's lead, many chemists in the the last half of the 19th century explored ways to create these longer-chain carbon substances from cheap, abundant materials. Among the likely raw materials for such experiments were the simple, inexpensive organic substances known as phenols and aldehydes.

Baekeland was drawn to these substances because of a famous 1872 experiment carried out by Adolf von Baeyer of Germany. Baeyer mixed a phenol together with another chemical called benzaldehyde, and he found that the fizzing, foaming reaction produced a strange, dark mass. The hard, porous material was almost impossible to work with. Chemists could not even pry it out of the glass test tubes, much less try to separate it into any pure substances so that it could be analyzed. Baeyer could see no point in wasting any time and effort on this chemical trash he had created. Other chemists who tried to combine phenol and aldehyde also quit in frustration.

Baekeland, however, thought that the product of one of the phenol-aldehyde reactions appeared to have the qualities of shellac—a natural product that had been commonly used for wood finishes and varnishes. A molded form of shellac had been developed for use as phonograph records, and electricians preferred this molded shellac to hard rubber for electrical insulation and fixtures.

There were two major problems with shellac. First, it could only be obtained from a small, red insect found in Southeast Asia, and so supplies of it were quite limited. The tremendous growth of the electronics industry was placing a great demand on these limited supplies. Second, shellac also was stable only at moderate temperatures. Its tendency to soften under heat and break down in cold temperatures made it a questionable material for electrical insulation. Baekeland realized that a commercial substitute for shellac that could stand up to heat and cold would be worth a fortune.

The problem was how to perfect this phenol-aldehyde reaction. There were so many variables involved. Baekeland had no theories that would predict his course of action, no way of knowing how much of each material to use, what temperatures and pressures would best aid the reaction, or what additives he should use to keep the reaction under control. All he could do was keep trying different experiments and making adjustments until he found something that worked.

Despite a rash of experiments, Baekeland could produce nothing but the kind of chemical trash that Baeyer had scoffed at. He could find nothing even close to the shellac substitute he was looking for. Working conditions in the Baekeland laboratory during this time were dreadful. Phenols and aldehydes are generally foul-smelling chemicals, and the stench became unbearable. After repeated experiments failed to produce the shellac substitute, some of Baekeland's assistants urged him to give up on the project.

But Baekeland was watching and learning from the failures, and he was able to eliminate some dead ends. Although it was commonly known that a hard material called celluloid could be made by adding nitric acid to cellulose, Baekeland found that, in this case, acid was not the answer. All it did was turn the phenol-aldehyde mixture into a sticky mess that dissolved in common solvents like alcohol. The addition of a base, a chemical that is in many ways the opposite of acid, however, resulted in a brittle product that could not be dissolved or melted. Because it was still a sludgelike mixture, it did not have much promise as a shellac. But Baekeland wondered if there were some way to get a purer, more uniform product that could make use of this extraordinary durability. If so, perhaps he could coat wood with it to obtain a stronger, weather-resistant product.

In June of 1907, while Baekeland was experimenting with his phenol-aldehyde mixture on some wood, he found that the reaction could be better controlled if he separated it into a three-stage process. He also discovered that the experts had been wrong in their ideas about controlling this reaction. Among those who had worked phenol-aldehyde combinations, it was commonly believed that the experiments had to be performed under low temperatures in order to keep the sizzling reaction under control. Baekeland thought that high temperatures might facilitate a better reaction, if only he could manage to keep the material from spluttering all over. He heated the mixture under pressure and added ammonia to reduce the foam.

Baekeland's controlled, high-temperature reaction was successful. It enabled him to prevent the formation of the gases that had muddied the phenol-aldehyde mixture. He tinkered with this new approach until he was able to obtain a more blended material at the end of the third stage of the reaction.

By this time, the chemist had begun to suspect that he was on to something far better than his original goal of a shellac substitute. From June 18 to June 20, 1907, Baekeland worked feverishly to perfect the reaction. He tried different methods, heating the mixture in sealed tubes, baking it in an oven of compressed air at temperatures of nearly 160° C. Eventually he produced a well-blended amber material that solidified into a hard, tough substance.

Baekeland recognized that the chemical name for his product, oxybenzylmethylen glycolanhydride, would not have much appeal to potential buyers. Instead, he called his new "oven-baked" concoction Bakalite, which was quickly changed to Bakelite.

Even while he was perfecting his process, he was thinking of ways to use this new material. The main advantage of Bakelite was that it was *thermosetting*. In other words, it could be easily molded into any shape, but after it had solidified, it could not be melted or softened again. Once hardened, it could be machined to any desired shape, and it was water-proof and resistant to heat, cold, and even acids. These characteristics, combined with the fact that it did not conduct electricity, made it a perfect insulator, far better than shellac or hard rubber—or any other material yet discovered.

Baekeland applied for a patent for his Bakelite on July 13, 1907, and he continued to perfect his process. He found that the main defect of Bakelite, its brittleness, could be remedied by adding a filler such as wood chips. On February 6, 1909, he was ready to introduce his discovery to the world. At a meeting of a chemistry society in New York, he described how "by the use of small amounts of bases, I have succeeded in preparing a solid initial condensation product, the properties of which simplify enormously all molding operations." He estimated that there were 43 different industries that could make use of Bakelite.

The invention of Bakelite could not have come at a better time for the electronics industry. Suddenly, a very workable, affordable material was available to form the many odd-shaped, insulated components needed in electrical products. It is difficult to imagine how a great number of products and businesses could have developed without Bakelite. Bakelite found its way into consumers' homes in the form of electrical plugs and sockets, pot handles, toasters, and circuit insulation. It made possible the production of inexpensive radios and so helped usher in the age of mass communication.

Perhaps its most dramatic effect was on transportation. Bakelite came along just as a new system of electronic ignition was developed for automobiles in 1910. Bakelite could be used for distributor heads, rotor arms, and many other small electrical parts that required some insulated covering. This inexpensive but durable material helped improve the quality of automobiles while cutting the cost down so that more people could afford them.

It turned out that Baekeland's estimate of the number of uses for Bakelite fell far short. His product eventually was used in such diverse products as airplane propellers, telephones, and, many years later, heat shields for spaceships.

As the U.S. patent-holder of this invention, Baekeland reaped the profits generated by this new material. His Bakelite Corporation expanded until, in 1922, it merged with two rivals in the growing chemical products industry. By the early 1930s, the Bakelite Corporation owned a 128-acre production plant and was churning out more than 30 million tons of finished product per year.

Baekeland continued to be active in the field of chemistry, contributing scientific papers throughout his life. To the end, his passion for his work overshadowed his personal relations. The great inventor not only avoided attention from strangers but frequently shunned the company of those close to him. He could spend weeks at a time working on his latest interest without bothering to see his family.

After selling his business interests to Union Carbide in 1939, Baekeland became increasingly eccentric. Although wealthy, he preferred soup or beans from a can for his meals. On hot days at his retirement home in Coconut Grove, Florida, he would walk fully clothed into his swimming pool.

Baekeland once expressed disappointment that his son did not follow him into chemistry to carry on his work. It is a surprising sentiment from one whose chief trait was that he never followed anyone or anything but the curiosity of his own mind. As for someone carrying on his work, there was hardly a shortage of followers. When Leo Baekeland died on February 23, 1944, at the age of 81, he had lived long enough to see the entire world reshaped by those who followed his footsteps.

Baekeland was the first to put together a series of small molecules in a chain to form a commercially useful artificial substance. His invention unleashed a flurry of chemical research into synthetic materials. In the 1930s, Wallace Carothers developed a synthetic material called nylon. The transparent stockings made from this material were so popular that four million pair were sold in the first four days the product was on the market. Polythene was developed by the British for military purposes and later modified for kitchenware and toys. Plexiglass, fiberglass, and many other raw materials that people had never before seen became available for their use.

The introduction of plastics, as this group of materials has come to be called, has not only changed the world, but has changed what is possible in the world. The possibilities of transportation, communication, construction, and manufacturing had always been limited by the materials at hand. The age of plastics, begun by Leo Baekeland, shattered those limits. When future inventors such as Aiken and Greatbatch sought materials out of which to build their products, there was a ready inventory available to them.

Chronology

November 14, 1863	Leo Hendrik Baekeland born in Ghent, Belgium
1882	graduates from University of Ghent
1887	holds position of professor of chemistry and physics at Government Normal School of Science in Bruges
1889	becomes assistant professor of chemistry at University of Ghent
1891	visits New York, stays on as a chemist for the E. & H.T. Anthony Company
1893	opens own consulting laboratory in New York City, develops Velox photographic paper
1899	sells rights to Velox invention to Eastman-Kodak for $1 million
1902	begins exploring idea of combining phenols and aldehydes
June 1907	perfects process for Bakelite
February 6, 1909	unveils Bakelite discovery to public
1910	organizes Bakelite Corporation
1939	sells business interests to Union Carbide
February 23, 1944	dies at the age of 81

Further Reading

Friedel, Robert. "The Plastics Man," *Science '84*, November 1984. One of a fascinating series of articles describing the most important technological breakthroughs of the 20th century. This focuses more on the actual invention than on Baekeland's life.

Thomas, Henry, and Dana Lee Thomas. *Living Advances in Science*, Freeport, N.Y.: Books for Libraries Press, 1972. This book includes an easy-reading chapter on Baekeland's life.

Robert Goddard & the Rocket

Robert Hutchings Goddard
(Library of Congress)

*A*t the root of all inventions, behind the nuts and bolts, the mathematical formulas and laws of physics, lies imagination.

Most of the inventors in this book drew on their imaginations in order to bring about stunning achievements in technology. Robert Goddard showed that invention can also work in reverse. He developed and tapped into his technical expertise in order to satisfy a desire of his imagination.

If the most striking common denominator of 20th-century inventors is that their work was their life, Goddard offers a more poetic version of that singleness of purpose. His dream was his life.

Goddard's dream was to send a rocket soaring into space, at a time when such a thing was considered impossible. His motivation for this strange goal was neither profit nor curiosity, but something more mystical. On October 19, 1899, 17-year-old Robert climbed a cherry tree to trim off the branches. While gazing from this height over the harvest fields below, he was struck with a vision of traveling into outer space.

What might have been a fleeting fantasy for most turned into an obsession for Goddard. He marked the date down in his calendar and declared, "I was a different boy when I descended the ladder." His life had a purpose that was to drive him until its end.

The "real" world is a seldom a safe haven for dreamers, and so it is not surprising that Goddard's quest was a struggle from start to finish. Far behind his classmates in his studies, Goddard was nearly 22 years of age before he earned his high school diploma. Working virtually alone, with little money and almost no recognition, he blazed a trail that all space exploration has since followed.

━━━━━━━━━

Robert Hutchings Goddard was born on October 5, 1882, in Worcester, Massachusetts, a city west of Boston. If ever a person was destined almost from the cradle to become an inventor it was Robert. He was no more than four or five when he dreamed up a scheme to electrically propel himself into space. His plan was to generate static electricity by scuffing the ground as he walked. Carrying a zinc rod from a battery to conduct the electricity, he then climbed a fence and jumped off. The youngster was convinced that his electric charge added several inches to his jump.

Robert seldom had a chance to exercise his creative mind in school as a boy. Serious, recurring illnesses confined him to his bed for months at a time, well over a year in one instance. There was nothing for him to do during these times other than to read, write, and think.

When Robert thought, he usually thought about creating something. He was constantly ordering equipment from mail-order catalogs and researching new experiments. When he was healthy, he spent his time performing experiments—such as trying to turn graphite into diamonds—flying kites, or inventing new gadgets.

Robert Goddard

Robert's father encouraged him in his interests by buying him such items as a telescope, microscope, and subscription to *Scientific American*.

At the age of 15, Robert decided to invent a sturdy balloon that would never deflate. His plan was to create a skin of thin aluminum and fill it with hydrogen. After considerable effort he was able to work the aluminum into the shape of a pillow. But the metal was still too heavy, and when he filled his balloon with hydrogen he could not get it to rise. Shortly thereafter, he read a recently published novel by H. G. Wells entitled *War of the Worlds*. The story about space invaders from another planet gave Robert's active imagination a whole new field in which to run. Goddard continued to read and even to write science fiction all of his life.

These fanciful stories primed him for his cherry tree experience in 1899. When he climbed down from the tree, he was determined to invent a means of traveling in space. At that time, no one had come close to demonstrating that it was possible to fly even an airplane, let alone a spaceship. Space travel was considered impossible because of the lack of air in outer space. Without air for a propeller to push against, how could there be any forward movement?

Goddard's first idea for hurling a rocket into space was to spin a projectile fast enough so that the centrifugal force, pushing it away from the center of its spin, would overcome the force of gravity. At the age of 19, he condensed some of his thoughts on space navigation into an article, which he submitted to a science magazine. Included in this article was the suggestion that a spaceship could be made up of a series of cannons, each cannon firing the remaining craft a little farther into space. This idea of a multistage rocket eventually became one of the basic techniques of space travel. The magazine, though, did not consider Goddard's effort worth publishing.

After building a few models to test his theories, he realized that he would have to become an expert in mathematics and physics if he wanted to overcome the barriers to space travel. Because of his many illnesses, Goddard's formal education had been haphazard. But after studying on his own for awhile, he made the courageous decision to enroll in high school in 1901, when he was already older than most high school graduates. Turning his full attention to his studies, Goddard soon caught and passed his younger classmates. He was enormously popular, twice elected class president, and graduated from South High School in Worcester at the top of his class.

While his academic life was flourishing, however, his dream was not. Goddard became so discouraged by his failed experiments that he was ready to admit that spaceflight was impossible. Shortly before graduating from South, he burned all of his notes in frustration. But two months later, Goddard was hatching new schemes for achieving his dream. He continued to be haunted by doubts during the next years but kept his spirits up by celebrating the anniversary of his cherry tree vision.

Goddard continued his studies at the Worcester Polytechnic Institute. It was there that he began to explore the possibilities of using rockets for space travel.

The idea of blasting into high altitudes with rocket propulsion was actually an ancient idea. The Chinese had built and fired rockets with gunpowder combustion chambers as early as the 13th century. By the 19th century, rockets were commonly used in European warfare. In the War of 1812, the British used rockets against American fortifications. Some of these missiles, weighing up to 60 pounds and with a range of 2 miles, helped inspire the words to the United States national anthem (" . . . the rockets red glare . . .") By the time Goddard was born, however, improvements in artillery technology had made rockets obsolete.

The further he looked into the situation, the more Goddard questioned the common assumption that rockets could not operate in airless space any more than could propellers. He set about accumulating enough knowledge so that he could begin figuring out whether it was mathematically possible to fire rockets into space. His notebooks were crammed with ideas and observations on rocketry, one of which was the notion of using liquid fuel for rocket power. As part of his spaceflight exploration, he also worked on experiments involving aircraft. Just four years after the Wright brothers' first successful flight, Goddard came up with a novel way to stabilize an aircraft by means of a gyroscope, a spinning disc mounted on a series of axes.

Rocket research, however, was not considered a proper subject for a scientist. In order to maintain his reputation as a serious student, Goddard studied electrical conductivity in preparation for a career in radio technology.

After graduating from Worcester Polytech in 1908, he continued his studies at another local school, Clark University. He obtained his doctorate in physics in 1911 and then went to Princeton

University on a research fellowship. There he continued to cover up his main interest under the respectable shield of radio research. While spending his days working on a device for long-distance radio transmission, which eventually led to a patent, Goddard stayed up at night working on rocket-propulsion problems.

With Goddard's poor health history, it was not long before the strain of living a double life caught up with him. He came down with tuberculosis and at one point was not expected to live more than two weeks. Goddard returned to Worcester, where he did little except rest and write about rockets for the next two years.

It was during this time of failing health that he began to make real progress in his reach for the stars. In 1912, he proved mathematically that rocket propulsion could work even without the presence of air, that is, in a vacuum, and that, with a proper motor, a rocket could be sent into space. A year later, he refined his calculations to show that it would be possible to build á 200-pound rocket capable of hurling a 1-pound load into space.

Goddard was rewarded in July of 1914 with the first of his patents dealing with space travel. One of these was for the multistage rocket, and the other for a mechanism to feed liquid fuel into a rocket combustion chamber.

The combination of rest and success provided a remarkable cure for his ills, and in 1914 he accepted a part-time job teaching at Clark University. He would continue to hold a faculty position at Clark until shortly before his death, and he was well-liked by his students. As a professor, he was careful to avoid preaching a "right" way of doing things. His own experience had taught him not to declare too strongly what was possible and impossible.

After teaching his classes during the day, Goddard would retreat into the privacy of his lab for more secret experiments on rockets. With each advance he made, he became more determined than ever to realize his dream. But the further he progressed, the more costly the experiments became. Goddard spent every spare cent he had on explosives and new lightweight metal alloys for constructing rockets, but it was not enough. Somehow he had to convince someone that space travel was not just a fantasy.

In 1916, he approached the Smithsonian Institution with a proposal that he had drawn up in 1913 called "A Method of Reaching Extreme Altitudes." Again he disguised his main goal of space travel by focusing on the value of a high-altitude rocket for studying the upper atmosphere. The Smithsonian was impressed by his presentation and agreed to provide $5,000 for his work.

That work was interrupted by United States involvement in World War I. Goddard offered his expertise in rockets to his country's armed forces, and he was put to work on developing new weapons. In 1918, he succeeded in perfecting a small, tube-launched, recoilless rocket, but the war ended before this could be put into production. Although Goddard's research led to the development of the bazooka, a hand-held rocket launcher, during World War II, he received little recognition for his work.

Goddard's secret explorations into space travel were exposed for the first time in January of 1920 when the Smithonian published his proposal on reaching extreme altitudes. The reaction of the press reinforced Goddard's desire to stay out of the public spot-light. Reporters ignored the solid technical foundation of his report and focused on a brief suggestion of Goddard's that it might be possible to send a rocket to the moon. Goddard was ridiculed as an impractical dreamer and nicknamed the Moon Man. *The New York Times* singled him out for harsh criticism. It said that Goddard's claim that a rocket could function in a vacuum demonstrated that he "only seems to lack the knowledge ladled out daily in high schools."

Stung by the criticism, Goddard returned to the secrecy of his lab for his experiments. There, he was continually frustrated by the problems with his solid fuel propellant. It was extremely difficult to regulate the flow of explosive substances such as gunpowder, and there were several accidents in which the combustion chamber was blown apart. The problems were great enough to drive Goddard back to his old idea of using liquid fuel.

Working with the aid of only a mechanic or two provided by Smithsonian funds, Goddard experienced one failure after another in his attempts to build a reliable fuel-feed system. Eventually he hit upon the idea of using liquid oxygen. When liquid oxygen warmed up and vaporized, it expanded, providing pressure. Goddard used this pressure to force the explosive mixture through the fuel line into the combustion chamber. A combination of gasoline and liquid oxygen was found to pack the explosive power needed, although the highly flammable material was extremely dangerous to work with. The solitary existence of this laboratory recluse was broken by Esther Kisk, a 17-year-old secretary in the administrative office at Clark who occasionally typed papers for him. Although Goddard was old enough to be her father, the two became close. Esther dropped out of college to marry Robert in 1924, and she began helping him with his work. Even she, however, thought her husband's ideas on space travel sounded farfetched.

The breakthrough came on Christmas Day of 1925. Goddard was able to ignite a lightweight rocket motor so that it lifted off the ground. Held back by restraining cables, it hovered above its stand for 24 seconds.

Encouraged by this result, Goddard set up a full-scale test run. On March 16, 1926, he and his assistant, Henry Sachs, loaded their equipment into a car and headed for a farm owned by Goddard's aunt in nearby Auburn, Massachusetts. They worked all morning long to set up a launchpad on the snow-covered ground near a cabbage patch.

Goddard poses with his rocket just before its first successful flight on March 16, 1926.
(Goddard Collection/Clark University)

Goddard's rocket was 10 feet long and weighed slightly more than 10 pounds. There was no casing or cover to enclose the parts. At the tip of the rocket Goddard had placed a small motor with an exhaust nozzle attached. The rear end of his rocket contained two tanks, one filled with gasoline, the other with liquid oxygen. These two fuels were fed into the motor through two long tubes that formed the sides of the rocket. When the rocket was ready for firing, an alcohol burner was lit under the oxygen tank to speed the vaporizing of the liquid oxygen.

Goddard was risking the last of his supply of liquid oxygen on this experiment. If the test failed, it would be at least a month before he could get a fresh supply. As Robert, Esther, and another professor watched from a safe distance, Henry Sachs touched a 6-foot torch to the igniter above the motor. The burning of the black powder in the igniter opened valves that allowed the liquid fuel to flow into the combustion chamber.

Sachs dashed for cover. The motor hissed and roared for a few agonizing seconds before the rocket shot into the air. It shot off with so little noise or sound that Goddard exclaimed that it seemed like magic. After a 2½ second ride carried it 41 feet into the air, the rocket plunged into the snow 184 feet away.

The test made a believer of Esther, but Goddard was not about to subject himself to further ridicule by going public with his results. Except for a private report that he sent to the Smithsonian, Goddard's rocket work went unnoticed until his fourth successful launch in 1929. Again, the attention was not favorable. A fiery impact on landing brought ambulances, police, and reporters scurrying to what they supposed was a plane crash. When the state fire marshal learned what Goddard was up to, he banned the physicist from further tests on the farm.

The new restrictions nearly forced Goddard to shut down his research. This time, though, he was saved by the famous aviator Charles Lindbergh, who had made the first solo flight across the Atlantic. Intrigued by news reports of the uproar over Goddard's flight, Lindbergh visited the rocket scientist. He was so impressed by Goddard's work that he arranged for private support of his work through the Daniel and Florence Guggenheim Foundation. With this backing, Goddard was able to devote full-time effort to his life-long dream. Except for a period in 1932–33 when the Great Depression forced a cutback in Guggenheim funds, Goddard was granted leave from Clark University from 1930 to 1942.

Robert Goddard

Thwarted by local restrictions in Massachusetts, Goddard scouted for a new launch site and settled on an isolated ranch near Roswell, New Mexico, in 1930. Although he now had a good supply of funds, Goddard did not change his research style. He had worked in secret for too long to set up any kind of team effort. Avoiding publicity and trusting only a few assistants, he labored in the desolate New Mexico desert, trying to build on the foundations he had established.

Failures were still the rule rather than the exception. Once he waited through six days of bad weather for a chance to demonstrate an improved design, only to find that the fuel lines were so clogged with ice that they could not function. On another occasion, a tornado destroyed both the launch tower and a carefully constructed rocket that was ready for launching.

Goddard rarely expressed disappointment over these calamities. In fact he liked to use the term *negative information* instead of failure. But he began to grow anxious over reports of rocket research overseas. In contrast to the United States' military authorities, who remained coolly indifferent to Goddard's work, officials in Germany and other countries were setting up large rocket research teams. Goddard rejected offers to share knowledge with these foreign scientists and began to work more diligently, sometimes day and night, on his research.

During his years on the bleak New Mexico plain, Goddard launched 34 rockets. With every new flight, he incorporated innovations, such as fuel injection, that drew him another step closer to the dream of space travel. In 1935, he fired off a rocket that traveled faster than the speed of sound. Eventually he launched a rocket to a height of nearly 9,000 feet, the closest he ever came to pulling free from the earth's gravity.

Again it was war that interrupted his research. When the United States was drawn into another world war in 1941, Goddard repeated his offer to help develop the rocket as a weapon. As usual, his ideas were rejected as impractical, and he was assigned instead to work on liquid-fuel motors. After a lifetime of closing in on an impossible dream, this work seemed a rather futile task. During the monotony of this effort, he kept a toehold on his cherished world of space exploration by writing science fiction stories.

Ironically, it was the enemy who put many of Goddard's ideas into practice. Near the end of World War II, German scientists introduced the V-2 rocket, commonly known as the buzz bomb. These high-altitude, unmanned, guided missiles were developed too late to turn the tide of war in Germany's favor, but they inflicted frightening damage on Great Britain.

When German scientists who had developed the V-2 came over to the Allied side at the end the war, they were asked to provide the details of their ingenious missile. One of the engineers replied that the Americans could have had that information any time they wanted by asking Goddard! The V-2 operated on the same principles as a rocket built by Goddard in 1939. The Germans had recognized early the value of rocketry and had been aware of Goddard since his publication of 1920.

But it was too late for Goddard to gain the recognition long due him. In the last year of his life, he noted that "the subject of projection from the earth, and especially mention of the moon, must still be avoided in dignified scientific and engineering circles." It is estimated that this failure of the United States to recognize Goddard's ideas set space exploration back 20 years.

Robert Goddard died on August 10, 1945, at the age of 62, following a throat operation. He never did achieve his ultimate dream, nor did he live to see the concept of space travel become a reality. But just 12 years after his death, the Soviet Union sent the first rocket into orbit around the earth. On July 20, 1969, 43 years after Goddard shot off his first rocket on his aunt's farm, United States astronaut Neil Armstrong stepped onto the surface of the moon. Scientists have recently sent out sophisticated equipment to Jupiter and beyond, and they have launched a new telescope that will be able to probe galaxies far beyond the range of earth-bound telescopes.

Responding to ridicule of his ideas, Goddard once wrote that "every vision is a joke until the first man accomplishes it." His life was a testament to the truth of this insight. Robert Goddard's stubborn pursuit of a dream led him to accumulate 214 patents pertaining to rockets. To this day, it is virtually impossible to design, build, or launch any space-exploration vehicle without infringing on those patents. One man, working almost completely by himself in an uncharted field, laid the foundation for the exploration of an entire universe.

Chronology

October 5, 1882	Robert Hutchings Goddard born in Worcester, Massachusetts
October 19, 1899	"cherry tree experience" motivates him to build rocket
1904	he graduates from high school at age 22
1908	graduates from Worcester Polytechnic Institute
1911	is awarded Ph.D. from Clark University
1914	collects first rocket patents
1916	gains backing of Smithsonian Institution for proposal of a method of obtaining extreme altitudes
1920	gains unwelcome notoriety when Smithsonian publishes his proposal
March 16, 1926	launchs first successful rocket at farm near Auburn, Massachusetts
1929	is banned by state fire marshal from doing further tests on the farm after fiery rocket crash
1930	moves rocket operations to Roswell, New Mexico
1935	fires rocket that breaks speed of sound
August 10, 1945	dies at age of 62

Further Reading

Lampton, Christopher. *Rocketry: From Goddard to Space Travel*. New York: Franklin Watts, 1988. An account of the history and physics of rocketry for young readers, starting with Goddard's contributions to the field.

Lehman, Milton. *This Higher Man: The Life of Robert H. Goddard*. New York: Da Capo Press, Inc., 1988. A detailed account of Goddard's life, updating *This High Man: The Life of Robert H. Goddard*, written 25 years earlier by the same author.

Lehman, Milton. *Robert H. Goddard: Pioneer Of Space Research*. New York: Da Capo Press, Inc., 1988. An in-depth (488 pages) discussion of Goddard's life and his contributions to space research and rocketry; written for an older audience.

Lomask, Milton. *Robert H. Goddard: Space Pioneer*. Dallas: Garrard Publishing Co., 1972. An account of Goddard's early contributions to space research; written for young readers.

Verral, Charles. *Robert Goddard: Father of the Space Age*. Englewood Cliffs, N.J.: Prentice-Hall, 1963. An account of Goddard's life for younger readers.

Vladimir Zworykin
& the Television

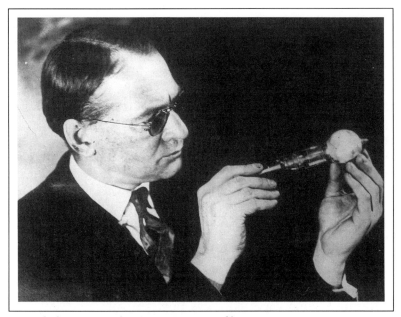

Vladimir Zworykin examines one of his inventions, a sensitive photoelectric tube.
(National Archives)

*T*he television industry has suffered the scorn of critics ever since the early days of commercial broadcasting. The quality of programming has led some to refer to television as a wasteland, or even an idiot box. But seldom have any of these attacks packed the wallop of the statements of a Russian immigrant named Vladimir Zworykin.

Despite the fact that he was a high-salaried employee of a television manufacturer, Zworykin frequently lashed out against the influence of television. "Television had a chance to become the greatest social force for good in this country," he said. "But it failed." Zworykin refused to watch the device, except when his wife alerted him to an educational show that might interest him.

His strong words were particularly ironic. Although television is a prime example of the corporate inventions that would come to dominate 20th-century inventory, Zworykin is the person generally considered most responsible for bringing television into the world.

Television is one result of Zworykin's dream of extending human vision. The electronics wizard spent decades in pursuit of an idea to extend the gift of sight beyond the limits of the human eye. He wanted humans to be able to see sights that were too far away, too small, too restricted, too dangerous for the average, person to see. In this task, he succeeded so well that *Newsweek* magazine said, "perhaps no man has contributed more to the electronic technology of the twentieth century."

While succeeding in his goals, he also brought about two other far-reaching developments that he could not have foreseen: the explosion of the entertainment industry and television's role as the instrument of democracy. For better or for worse, Zworykin's brainchild has become a major influence on the lives of billions of people.

Vladimir Kosma Zworykin was born on July 30, 1889, in the town of Murom, Russia, 200 miles east of Moscow. He was the youngest of seven children born to Kosmo and Elaine Zworykin, a well-to-do couple who operated boats on the Oka River. From the age of nine, Vladimir spent his summers working odd jobs on the boats. One of his tasks was to help repair electrical equipment, which he found fascinating.

After graduation from high school, Zworykin entered the University of St. Petersburg looking for a way to combine a career with his interest in electricity. The lectures on physics were so intriguing that Zworykin decided to become a physicist. His practical-minded father, however, could not see how this high-minded physics was going to put food on the table. He insisted that Vladimir concentrate on what he considered a more useful trade—engineering.

Vladimir agreed and transferred to the Imperial Institute of Technology in St. Petersburg in 1906. It was there that he met a man who had a "vision" about vision. Professor Boris von Rosing, who was in charge of laboratory projects at the institute, had an idea that he could transmit pictures by electric wire. It had been well established by this time that sounds could be transmitted electronically. The volume and pitch of the sound produced variations in electrical current. This current could travel across a wire to a receiver that could translate the current back into sound. In fact Guglielmo Marconi had recently shown that one did not need even an electrical wire—sounds could be transmitted and captured through the air.

Further, in 1884 a German named Paul Nipkow had patented a device that could transmit extremely crude pictures. Nipkow's idea was to put a great deal of light on the target object. This lighted target would then be scanned by a spinning disk that was punctured with a pattern of holes. The varying amount of light coming through the holes could be translated by a photocell into electrical current.

Professor Rosing was out to improve on this system, and Zworykin was assigned to help him out. For several years they worked on the project, blowing their own glass to fashion tubes and hand-building all the equipment. Even though they failed to come up with a workable system, Zworykin thoroughly enjoyed the experience. He also gained from Rosing the knowledge that a cathode-ray tube could play a useful role in any future efforts to produce electronic pictures. A cathode-ray tube was a vacuum tube that produced high-speed electrons, small negatively charged particles, in a stream.

Zworykin received his engineering degree in 1912, but he could not rid himself of the desire to probe into the uncharted realms of physics. He traveled to Paris to study X rays and was there when World War I broke out in 1914. Immediately he returned to Russia where he was recruited into the army.

His assigned post at Grodno, near the Polish border, had no radio transmitter. Upon finding that Zworykin had an electrical engineering degree, his officers ordered him to build a transmitting station. By the next day, Zworykin was sending out messages. He was then transferred to a radio school for communications officers. After a year and a half of study, he won a commission and a job teaching electronics. At the same time, he married Tatiana Vasilieff.

In 1917, the Russian Revolution broke out, plunging the country into chaos. Zworykin saw no hope of getting on with his engineering work in the middle of this upheaval, and he asked for permission to leave the country. When he finally persuaded the authorities to let him go, the United States denied him a visa to enter the country.

Fearful of suffering the same fate as Professor Rosing, who was arrested and sent into exile, Zworykin fled into the countryside. After some months of wandering, he ended up in the northern port town of Archangel. An Allied military force happened to be in the harbor, and Zworykin saw this as his chance. He persuaded the American officials of the expedition that he was an electrical engineer with some valuable skills to contribute to the United States. Zworykin was taken on board and brought as far as London. From there he sailed to the United States, arriving in 1919, and he and his wife became U.S. citizens.

After landing, he worked for a time as a bookkeeper in the Russian Embassy before joining the Westinghouse Company in Pittsburgh, Pennsylvania. Throughout the drastic changes in his life, Zworykin had never lost his enthusiasm for his pet project, and he approached Westinghouse engineers with his plans for an electric television. Westinghouse showed no interest in his ideas, however, and Zworykin quit. He went to work for an electronics company in Kansas while he tried to refine his ideas for a television.

He returned to Westinghouse, in 1923, and a new manager allowed him the freedom to work on technology related to television, including radio tubes and photoelectric cells. What little spare time he had was taken up with classes at the University of Pittsburgh, where he obtained his Ph.D. in 1926.

Since Zworykin had last tinkered with Rosing's television experiments, Scottish engineer A. A. Campbell-Swinton had made a few technological advances in this area. Among these were the use of cathode-ray tubes in both the transmitter and the receiver. Campbell-Swinton's most ingenious idea was to focus the desired scene onto a plate fixed inside a cathode-ray tube. The front side of the plate would be filled with dots of photoelectric metal—metal that gave off electrons when light was shined on it.

The metallic dots would give off a certain amount of electrons, depending on how much light was shining on them. This would build up a positive charge on the metal coating on the back of the plate. A beam of electrons could then scan this stored variety of charges. The result would be that the picture would be recorded on the metal plate as a sequence of voltages, and this sequence of voltages would be sent out as the signal. A cathode-ray receiver, located in the actual television set, could then translate this electrical signal back into a visual image.

While the reasoning behind this was masterful, there was no assurance that such a device could be built. Campbell-Swinton conceded that the whole concept would take an enormous amount of experimentation and would probably undergo some drastic changes in design before it would ever work. One of the main obstacles was the creation of those photoelectric dots. In order to get a clear picture, the plate would need to register thousands, perhaps millions, of minute voltage changes. Further, these dots would have to be insulated. How could anyone possibly develop a way to put that many insulated dots onto a plate? Even if they could, could it ever be made practical, so that television would be affordable?

The problems standing in the way of this electronic technology were great enough to persuade a number of inventors to return to Nipkow's idea of a mechanical television. Englishman John L. Baird and American Charles F. Jenkins both created a television in the 1920s based on the mechanical spinning disk. Both models, however, required intense light in order to produce a hazy, fuzzy image. Zworykin knew that mechanical scanning devices could not come close to matching the speed of an electrical scanner. The more variations in light that could be detected by a transmitting device, the better the chance of producing a clear picture, and so he remained convinced that electricity was the way to go.

Working on his own, Zworykin constructed a form of television transmitting tube based on some of Campbell-Swinton's concepts. This device, which he called an iconoscope, was the forerunner of today's television camera.

Zworykin applied for a patent on his iconoscope in December 1923. At about that time he eagerly demonstrated his new device to his superiors at Westinghouse. While the engineer proudly showed off his breakthrough, his audience looked on in bewilderment. All they could see were dark, shadowy images of a cross. Zworykin was asked what he thought he could do with this iconoscope. The possibilities were unlimited, according to the inventor. Television could radically improve civilization by bringing once- inaccessible knowledge and culture into the homes of everyday people. His enthusiasm over the possibilities of "extending man's sight" into all areas of the universe did not produce the desired effect. Westinghouse engineers pointed out that his electronic device could not even match the fuzzy standards of the mechanical televisions being produced. A few days later, they politely suggested that Zworykin "do something more useful" while working on company time.

But Zworykin continued to tinker with his system over the next few years. He realized that the iconoscope that he had invented was only half the battle. It would be worthless to develop a reliable method of transmitting pictures into electricity without a suitable device to translate the electronic signals back into clear images. After experimenting with various forms of cathode-ray tubes, Zworykin finally achieved success in 1929. He developed the kinescope, a special cathode-ray tube that could use a beam of electrons to form an image on a screen. With an iconoscope at one end of the process, sending a picture, and his new kinescope at the other end to receive it and recreate the image, he had a complete system for transferring pictures electronically.

This time Zworykin thought his improvements were impressive enough to risk a public demonstration. At a convention of radio engineers in November 1929, he showed off his new kinescope. This time he attracted more than just yawns. Among those who saw Zworykin's work was Radio Corporation of America (RCA) executive David Sarnoff. Coincidentally, Sarnoff was also a Russian immigrant.

After considering Zworykin's project, Sarnoff asked him how close he was to developing a practical television. How much time and money would it take? Ever the optimist, Zworykin estimated that he could get it done with another year and a half of work. It would not be cheap, though. Choosing what he thought was an impressive figure, Zworykin guessed that RCA might have to pump $100,000 into the project before they had a workable model.

Sarnoff decided to go ahead with the development of the television and assigned Zworykin to a position as director of electronic research at RCA. He had caught Zworykin's vision of the future, and he was convinced that television had unlimited potential. He was willing to bet the future of RCA on Vladimir Zworykin's shadowy picture box. Fortunately for Zworykin, Sarnoff was not a man who gave up easily. The inventor's estimate turned out to be laughable. At a time when many businesses were struggling through the Great Depression, RCA had to throw millions of dollars into a project that produced painfully slow results. Zworykin later modestly described himself as "only the dreamer" and gave Sarnoff the credit for making the dream come true.

Vladimir Zworykin

While working on various aspects of television, Zworykin developed a number of related ideas that would one day prove useful. In 1929, even before the black-and-white television had been refined, he patented some concepts that would lead to development of color television. In 1930, he experimented with an infrared image tube. By using invisible infrared light and then assigning visible colors to various invisible wavelengths, Zworykin eventually came up with a device that enabled people to see in the dark. This "sniperscope" gave American soldiers an important advantage in World War II.

Although Sarnoff had confidence in his electronic wizard, RCA did not place all its bets on Zworykin. In their determination to produce a television product, they also explored some of the mechanical methods of scanning.

Zworykin's biggest breakthrough in television engineering was solving the problem of the insulated photoelectric islands. The solution turned out to be wonderfully simple. He sifted silver-oxide powder onto a thin sheet of mica, an insulating material. The mica was then heated to drive the oxygen out of the powder. This left behind millions of tiny silver specks, each one insulated by mica. Zworykin then treated the silver with cesium oxide to make it photosensitive.

In 1932, RCA was ready to run a test pitting Zworykin's electronic television against the best mechanical system. Zworykin's improved iconoscope easily outperformed the mechanical model. The following year, RCA was ready for a field test. They were able to transmit images from an iconoscope at RCA's Camden laboratory to a kinescope located 4 miles away, in Collingswood, New Jersey. The receiving set used a mirror to reflect the image from a 9-inch picture tube onto a screen. The success of this experiment convinced Zworykin that his dream of an electronic "extension of the eye" had been achieved. The problem of amplifying the electronic signals so they could travel to a receiver many miles away had already been solved by the radio industry. All that was left was for technicians to fine-tune Zworykin's process and package it into a consumer product.

It took five more years before the first televisions began to reach the market. In 1938, a mobile television unit in New York City happened upon a fire and filmed the first unscheduled news event. Within a year, there were 23 television stations gearing up for broadcast. Then, just as the new industry was getting started, it

This 1939 RCA Victor television has a 9-inch kinescope, reproducing images 5½" X 7¼" for direct viewing.
(Courtesy of David Sarnoff Research Center)

was tied up in bureaucratic wrangling over how to regulate the air waves.

Commercial television did not receive approval from the Federal Communications Commission (FCC) until 1941. By that time, the United States had more immediate concerns, with war brewing in both the Atlantic and the Pacific. During the war, Zworykin and his team of electrical engineers produced a picture tube that was 100 times more sensitive than the former version.

Only by a rare stroke of luck did Zworykin live to see the effects of his invention. During a company-sponsored trip in 1939, he was ready to sail home from Lebanon when he remembered a humiliating moment from his initial voyage to the United States. As an officer, Zworykin was given first-class passage on that 1919 trip. He did not have any formal clothes at that time and he never forgot the embarrassment of having to sit down to dinner among well-dressed first-class passengers without a dinner jacket.

As the SS *Athenia* was about to leave Lebanon, Zworykin remembered that he had no formal jacket this time, either. Rather than suffer a repeat of his earlier embarrassment, he postponed his trip until he could purchase a jacket. The *Athenia* left without him and was sunk off the Irish coast by a German torpedo.

By 1946, all the technical and governmental barriers standing in the way of television had been removed. After nearly two decades of research and $50 million in development costs (500 times the price tag that Zworykin had estimated), a 10-inch model black-and-white television was on the market for $375. Despite the steep price, more than 130,000 television sets were sold in the next year in the United States. Two years later, more than three and half million sets were in use in the country.

In 1953, the FCC approved the production of color television sets, and these arrived on the market the following year. By this time, only eight years after televisions were readily available, 60 percent of U.S. homes owned at least one black-and-white set. Television shows could reach an audience of 40 million viewers at one time.

While Zworykin looked on in despair, his television was turned into an entertainment gold mine. It turned out that television had the profound impact on society that he had foreseen, only it was not the type of impact he had in mind. Instead of elevating the level of awareness and knowledge, Zworykin saw television as a device that was allowing people to waste their minds on froth and trivia and was bombarding the country with sales pitches.

Throughout his life, Zworykin opposed by word and deed the abuse of his invention. While denouncing commercial television and proclaiming that it was not worth watching, he kept searching for ways to bring back his dream of what television was supposed to be. He never thought of television as anything but the eye that helped people see things that their own eyes were incapable of seeing.

In the 1930s, he predicted that television cameras could be put in the nosecones of missiles to guide them to their targets. Now such guidance systems are standard military equipment. In the 1950s, he spoke about the wealth of scientific information that could be beamed back to earth from satellites. The televised pictures that reached the earth from the moon and Mars and planets beyond brought Zworykin enormous satisfaction.

Some of Zworykin's most useful adaptations of his seeing eye were in the area of microscopes, which he began working on in 1937. Visible light is capable of magnifying an object 2,500 times. The limiting factor is the length of the light waves. Objects smaller than light waves could not be seen. Zworykin had spent some time working with infrared waves, which are longer than visible light. In order to see into the microscopic world, he turned to the opposite end of the spectrum—ultraviolet rays, which are shorter than visible light waves.

Zworykin eventually achieved startling magnification by using an electromagnetic tube to focus short-wave rays at an object. By assigning visible colors to the different wavelengths of invisible light, he could produce a visible picture. With such a microscope, humans could even see the workings of the cells of their own bodies. Zworykin directed the team that pioneered the electron microscope, a device that could make incredibly small objects visible by focusing electron beams instead of light. Electron microscopes have penetrated the dark frontier of the microscopic world to bring about advances in medicine and microbiology.

After 25 years as the head of RCA's Electronics Laboratories, Zworykin retired in 1954. But he never retired from work. As he said late in life, "I've worked all my life—I can't stop." He continued to work on his ambitious electrical projects, including a search for an energy generator that could be placed in each home, until his death on July 30, 1982.

By the time of his death, the monster that he had created had grown almost beyond belief. More than 500 million television sets were in use around the world, piping American culture into the some of the poorest slums in the Third World. Television had joined family, friends, school, and church as one of the major influences on a child's life, and some estimate that it has gravitated toward the top of that list.

While debate continues as to the exact effects of television on society, it is known that U.S. children spend an average of more than 3½ hours a day with the "extended eye"—3½ hours a day more than children spent with television prior to 1940.

While many echo Zworykin's disappointment with the effects of television, the invention has also produced some obvious good. Television's impact was demonstrated vividly during the great upheaval in Eastern Europe during 1989. Television provided the common people with access to information. They could see the advantages of free democracies in other parts of the world and could gain inspiration from the example of those in neighboring countries who were demanding freedom. Television's influence in world affairs is considered so great that the press began referring to it as "The Third Superpower." It may not have turned out the way Zworykin had planned, but there can be no doubt that the world has become a different place since television arrived.

Chronology

July 30, 1889	Vladimir Kosma Zworykin born in Murom, Russia
1906	enters Imperial Institute of Technology at St. Petersburg, where he is introduced to television pioneer Boris von Rosing
1912	obtains engineering degree from the Imperial Institute
1914–17	serves in Russian army
1919	settles in the United States and begins working as an electrical engineer
1923	develops the iconoscope, an electric television camera
1926	receives Ph.D. from the University of Pittsburgh
1929	develops the kinescope, an electric television picture receiver; gains backing of RCA's David Sarnoff
1932	first successful field test of the Zworykin system is conducted
1941	Federal Communications Commission approves black-and-white television
1953	FCC approves color television
1954	Zworykin retires from RCA
July 30, 1982	dies at age of 93

Further Reading

Fink, Donald G. "The Tube," *Science '84*, November 1984. One of a fascinating series of articles describing the most important technological breakthroughs of the 20th century. This focuses more on the actual invention of the television than on Zworykin's life.

Fireman, Judy. *The TV Book*. New York: Workman, 1977. This lavishly illustrated book concentrates on early television programing, but includes a section on Zworykin as well as information on television technology.

Those Inventive Americans. Washington: National Geographic Society, 1971. Although shelved in the adult section of the library, this book is very readable for young adult audiences. It includes information on Lawrence and Shockley, as well as Zworykin.

Ernest Lawrence
& the Cyclotron

Ernest Orlando Lawrence
(Courtesy of Oak Ridge National Laboratory)

*T*here is a 20th-century invention that has been used only twice for the purpose for which it was intended. During the past 46 years it has sat around unused, except for an occasional test run. Only a relative handful of people have ever had any contact with it.

Yet this idle device has been one of the dominant creations of our age. It has cast a terrifying shadow on nearly every political dispute in the world. Potentially, it could have far more impact on the human race than all other inventions put together. This invention is the nuclear bomb , and it can do more than alter the world—with the push of a button, it can utterly destroy it.

There is no one inventor of nuclear weapons, and, in fact, an act of Congress forbids the assigning of patents for the creation of atomic weapons. So many scientists and engineers contributed to the formation of the original atomic bomb that it would be unfair to highlight any one of them as the originator.

But there was one person who dreamed up a machine that was able to crack open the tiny building blocks of the universe known as atoms. With his atom-smashing cyclotron, Ernest Lawrence provided the tool that enabled scientists to explore the unimaginable power stored in these invisible nuclei—power that could be used for good as well as for evil.

Ernest Orlando Lawrence was born on August 8, 1901, in Canton, South Dakota, the older of two sons born to Carl and Gunda Lawrence. Young Ernest was surrounded by intellectual influences. Both of his parents originally taught school, and his father became superintendent of schools in Canton, and eventually a college president. One of Ernest's best friends, Merle Tuve, went on to become one of the United States' leading physicists. As youngsters, Ernest and Merle fed each other's interest in science. They enjoyed building gliders, taking apart automobiles, and experimenting with radios. Ernest gained a reputation for being able to fix almost anything.

According to his mother, Ernest was "born grown up," with an unusual ability to size up people and situations. He was always in a hurry and was able to complete high school at the age of 16 because of the extra course loads he took. The serious side of his personality became more pronounced after the death of his 12-year old cousin from leukemia. Shaken by the tragedy, both Ernest and his younger brother John resolved to become doctors to do what they could to save lives.

Because of Ernest's young age, his parents started him out at a small, private college, St. Olaf College, in Northfield, Minnesota. He was not an exceptional student. English was never his strong subject, and he barely passed one of his math courses at St. Olaf. After studying there in 1918 and 1919, he transferred to the pre-medical program at South Dakota State University (SDSU). One of his advisers at SDSU saw that Lawrence had an exceptional gift for physics and he encouraged his student to develop that gift. Lawrence held firm with his goal of medical school, but after he graduated from South Dakota State in 1922, he was offered a fellowship to study for his master's degree at the University of Minnesota. It was there that he was captivated by the mysteries of the atom.

It had long been believed that atoms were the smallest particles in the universe, in fact the name *atom* means "that which cannot be divided." But experiments in the late 19th century had shown that atoms were made up of smaller parts: a tiny nucleus in the center and a "shell" of even tinier electrons that revolved around the nucleus.

In 1919, British physicist Ernest Rutherford demonstrated that even the nucleus of atoms could be split apart. Other physicists followed Rutherford's lead of bombarding atoms with radioactive particles in an attempt to crack open the atom. Unfortunately, Rutherford's discovery was of little practical use. The radium he used to produce the high-energy particles was scarce, and these particles did not strike the target often enough to provide measurable results. The problem was that a nucleus makes up only a tiny portion of the atom's volume. As Lawrence later said, trying to hit this miniscule target was like "trying to hit a fly in a cathedral."

Other attempts to fire particle "bullets" at atoms could not accelerate the bullets fast enough to build up the energy needed to succeed. If a scientist used particles with a positive charge (called protons), these were repulsed by the protons in the nucleus. If negatively charged particles (electrons) were used, they were repulsed by the electrons surrounding the atom. If a particle bullet had enough energy to get past these forces, it still had to overcome the most powerful force in the universe—the force holding a nucleus together.

Lawrence was introduced to the realm of particle bombardment in his studies of the photoelectric effect. This area of physics deals with the energizing of atoms by adding or removing electrons, and the standard procedure for manipulating electrons was by the use of high-speed particles. Even though he was not directly involved in atom-smashing research, he joined many physicists in wondering what it would take to pry open a nucleus.

Lawrence earned his master's degree at the University of Minnesota, then followed one of his professors to the University of Chicago, and then to Yale University in 1924. At one point, Lawrence debated giving up on a physics career, in the belief that he was not smart enough to learn what he needed to know. One day, however, he accompanied an influential United States physicist on a tour of Yale. The man asked a great many of what Lawrence considered to be "foolish" questions. By the time the tour was over, Lawrence decided he had underestimated his own intelligence and resolved to continue with the program. He completed his doctorate in 1925 and stayed on at Yale as a member of the faculty.

Both the integrity and the stubborness that characterized all of Lawrence's efforts are illustrated by an incident that occurred while he was teaching at Yale. Lawrence did not have much money and did not own an automobile. A parent of one of his students offered to buy Lawrence a new car if Lawrence would give his boy special treatment so that he could pass the course. Lawrence not only refused but went right out and bought himself a car that he could not afford.

Lawrence was not satisfied with his classroom duties at Yale. He was well aware that many of the most spectacular breakthroughs in physics over the years had been made by young men. As he approached his late 20s, Lawrence felt that time was running out on him to make an impact in his field. He was restless to go to a place that would allow him to do more private research.

In 1928, the University of California at Berkeley was trying to upgrade its physics department. Many of Lawrence's associates were stunned to learn that he had accepted a cut in pay in order to transfer to a less respected institution. But Lawrence was eager for a fresh start and new freedom to try out some of his ideas. He had become convinced that there were great discoveries to be made concerning the inner workings of the atom.

One day in the spring of 1929, he stumbled across an article that would change his life and the world. Browsing through scientific journals, as he often did in his spare time, Lawrence came across a brief report by Norwegian scientist Rolf Wideroe. This paper was about experiments that Wideroe had performed with positive ions, which are atoms that have lost electrons and so have a positive charge.

The text was in German and Lawrence was not able to understand much of it. But what caught his eye was a diagram on the first page of the article. The illustration showed that when potassium ions were hit twice by a certain voltage source, they moved at twice the energy level of that voltage source.

As soon as Lawrence saw the diagram, he realized that this could be the secret to breaking open atomic nuclei. Other researchers had toyed with the idea of accelerating atomic particles to high energy levels by giving them a series of pushes. But no one had worked out just how this could be done. Wideroe's diagram gave Lawrence the answer. A quick set of calculations showed Lawrence that a voltage source should be able to increase the energy level of a particle every time it was applied. If that was true, why not construct a circular track that would keep funneling the particle past the voltage source? By that method, eventually you should be able to get extremely high energy particles with just a modest voltage source.

Lawrence sketched out a plan that called for magnetic fields to steer the charged particles into traveling a circular course. He was so certain of the importance of what he had that he told a colleague that night that he had found a way to break apart atoms. Excited though he was, he went home to bed to sleep on his ideas. When he awoke and reevaluated his idea, he found it as exciting as ever. Astounded by his good fortune, he kept chortling about the results of his equations. He kept repeating to his friends that there was no limit to the speeds at which particles could be accelerated. He had beaten his self-imposed 30-year deadline for making a breakthrough—he was certain he was going to be famous!

Having an idea and putting it into practice, however, are two different things. Unable to excite anyone else about his discovery, Lawrence did not immediately pursue his idea. During the Christmas holidays that year, he visited his brother out East. There he was introduced to Nobel Prize winner Otto Stern. When he described his ideas to Stern, the physicist replied that Lawrence should be working on the proposal, not just dreaming about it.

With this encouragement, Lawrence set out to see if he could build a circular particle accelerator, as he called it. If he failed, it would not be for lack of effort. Like the other inventors in this book, Lawrence was so involved in his work that he frequently considered eating and sleeping to be irritating interruptions. He occasionally played tennis, but it was more for fitness than fun, and on most days he was hard at work from 8 A.M. until midnight.

Working on a shoestring budget, Lawrence began constructing his machine out of coffee cans, plate glass, sealing wax, and scraps of laboratory equipment. At a September 1930 meeting of the Academy of Sciences, Lawrence showed off an odd-looking little contraption consisting of a 4-inch brass chamber connected to

Ernest Lawrence

Lawrence holds the tiny machine in which he
first demonstrated the principles of
the cyclotron.
(Courtesy of Lawrence/Berkeley Laboratory)

several arms that were mounted between poles of an electromagnet. Crude as the device was, an electrometer showed that it was producing ions that traveled at higher energy levels than was contained in the electromagnetic field. This proved to Lawrence's satisfaction that the principle of his accelerator was correct. It was just a matter of refinement before they had a workable machine.

While Lawrence was in these early stages of inventing, one of his students was looking for a project to work on for his graduate studies. Lawrence persuaded M. Stanley Livingston to take up the challenge of working with him on the accelerator. Livingston was able to solve some of the engineering problems that had stood in Lawrence's way, and it was Livingston who did much of the actual hands-on work of building the device.

Many frustrating months passed, however, before Lawrence's team produced a working accelerator. Lawrence's own curiosity provided some of those frustrations. He loved to manipulate controls and had a habit of testing every device by pushing it to its limit. During one such test, he shattered the glass plates of one of his earlier models. After their boss broke a distressing amount of equipment, his assistants began to put governors on the controls so that they could not be pushed past a certain level.

Gradually, a workable accelerator was developed. On January 2, 1931, a tiny, 4½-inch cyclotron accelerated particles to 80,000 volts of energy, using a 2,000 volt magnetic field. This was still far short of the desired energy level for an atom smasher, and very few ions were actually accelerated to that level. Lawrence knew he needed millions of particle bullets in order to be sure of hitting his "fly in the cathedral." Yet it confirmed that Lawrence was headed in the right direction.

The basic design of this machine centered on a large, hollow, circular disk that was divided in half so that it formed two D-shaped semi-circles. A current was applied to these two "dees," as they were called, so that they contained opposite charges. These dees were then sandwiched between two large magnets.

Protons were directed to the gap between the dees, where they were attracted to the negative side and repelled by the positive side. The force field supplied by the magnets caused the particles to move in a circle that sent the particles back into the gap between the dees. This time when the particles arrived, the alternating electric current reversed, kicking the particles into the opposite dee. Every time the proton crossed the gap between these dees, the current was reversed, giving the particles another energy boost. With each energy boost, the particles traveled in a larger circle. Finally the high-speed particles would reach an opening in the machine that would aim them at a target.

Lawrence called his machine a *magnetic resonance accelerator*. His assistants enjoyed teasing him by calling it their own pet name—the *cyclotron*. Eventually the simpler name caught on. Even Lawrence had to yield to prevailing opinion, and the family of circular particle accelerators became known as cyclotrons.

While supervising these experiments, Lawrence somehow found time to carry on a cross-country courtship. In June of 1931, he was engaged to Molly Blumer, the daughter of a Yale professor. The two married in May of 1932 and eventually raised six children.

Ernest Lawrence

By the next year, Lawrence's team had scaled up to an 11-inch cyclotron. When Livingston ran a test on it, he discovered that it was accelerating a large number of protons to energy levels of more than a million volts. Lawrence, who was known for his outbursts of enthusiasm, rushed into the room and began dancing for joy. He applied for a patent on January 16, 1932, but he was far more excited about what he could do with his machine than in any money he might make from it. In fact when he was finally awarded his patent, he declined to exercise the rights.

Lawrence was riding a wave of good fortune that year. The recognition that he had anticipated that night in the library came pouring down on him. Not only were his fellow scientists familiar with Lawrence's efforts, but profiles on him were written up in general newspapers and magazines throughout the country. He was able to attract funding for his research from private sources. University of California-Berkeley officials gave him a small building in which to do his work.

But Lawrence was plotting even greater achievements. In order to reach the particle acceleration levels he desired, though, he needed to come up with an enormous magnet. Luck was with Lawrence, for he was able to locate a spare, 85-ton electromagnet not far from his laboratory. The magnet which had originally been built for a radio transmission technology that was now obsolete, was rusting away in a dump.

While Lawrence concentrated on building bigger and more powerful cyclotrons that year, British researchers proved that existing particle accelerators were strong enough to break open small atoms. A linear, or straight-line, accelerator was able to convert lithium atoms into helium, meaning that the number of protons in the nucleus was reduced by one. Upon learning this, Lawrence's team began their own bombardments. In September of 1932, they succeeded in breaking open atoms with the cyclotron.

Lawrence was sitting on top of the world when he made an appearance at the Chicago World's Fair in 1933. It was there, however, that he declared that the atomic particle recently discovered by James Chadwick was not really a neutron, as Chadwick claimed. Rather, Lawrence's analysis showed that it was just a combined proton and electron that canceled each other's charge. Lawrence was later sorely embarrassed to discover that Chadwick was right and he was wrong. Lawrence then redoubled his efforts at unlocking the secrets of the nucleus.

Lawrence's wife learned that living with a dedicated scientist is not easy. Molly Lawrence had to learn to sleep to the sound of a buzzing radio. Her husband was so intent on keeping tabs on his accelerator that he developed his own 24-hour-a-day monitoring service. He kept a bedside radio tuned to a frequency over which he broadcast the sound of his machine. If the noise stopped, Lawrence rushed to the telephone to find out what was the matter.

Once Lawrence had established the principle of the cyclotron, rapid improvements led to astounding results. In 1933, he constructed a 27½-inch accelerator. When Irene Joliet-Curie and her husband Frederic discovered in January of 1931 that radioactivity, the property of emitting radiation, could be artificially produced in an element by shooting atomic particles into nuclei, Lawrence's new machine provided a powerful tool for creating radioactivity. Later that year, his laboratory created a new radioactive element by bombarding carbon atoms with deuterium ions. The addition of a proton in the nuclei changed the carbon atoms into unstable, radioactive nitrogen 13 atoms.

In 1936, Lawrence unveiled a more powerful weapon in the assault on the atom, a 37-inch cyclotron capable of accelerating particles to energies of eight million volts. Such machines were capable of the most incredible feats, and Lawrence and his colleagues were like kids frolicking on a new playground. Almost gleefully, they bombarded one element after another. They could form radioactive isotopes, or slight variations, of most known elements. Occasionally they could imbed particles in a nucleus to form entirely new elements.

Physicists have said that the cyclotron revealed as many secrets in its time as the microscope had in its. Within eight years following the invention of the cyclotron, more than 360 radioactive isotopes were created, a third of them in Lawrence's own laboratory. The discovery of these isotopes was probably one of the most personally satisfying of Lawrence's achievements. In 1935, his brother John began looking into the effects of high-energy particles on human tissue. He was able to transfer this knowledge into a new radiation therapy to attack cancer cells. One of his first patients was his own mother, who lived another two decades following radiation treatment of her pelvic cancer.

The cyclotron also uncovered a great deal of information about the structure of atomic nuclei. Data gained from cyclotrons enabled scientists to put together accurate charts describing the various elements. The significance of the information gained with

Lawrence's cyclotron was recognized by the Royal Swedish Academy of Science, which awarded him the Nobel Prize in physics in 1939.

At about the same time, however, scientists began to uncover the dark side of this new scientific wonderland. German scientists discovered that uranium could be not only altered but actually split. In theory, this could set off a chain reaction that would release unimaginable power. The idea of Nazi Germany wielding such power pushed U.S. scientists into all all-out effort to develop an atomic bomb for their country before German scientists did.

Lawrence's feelings on the subject were clear. "I feel strongly, that anyone who hesitates on a vigorous, all-out effort on uranium assumes a grave responsibility." Working with a 4,500-ton, 184-inch cyclotron, Lawrence devoted himself to the atomic bomb effort. In 1941, his laboratory produced the first significant amount of enriched uranium 235. By the summer of 1945, his laboratory had made enough of this material to equip an atomic bomb. In August of 1945, a lonely New Mexico desert erupted in a horrendous blast. This successful test of an atomic bomb ended the era of innocence in atomic research. The almost unlimited

One of Lawrence's last projects was this Bevatron, the largest particle accelerator at the Lawrence/Berkeley Laboratory.
(Courtesy of Lawrence/Berkeley Laboratory)

power of the atom could now be used to destroy as well as to serve humans.

As U.S. military forces prepared to use the bomb against Japan, Lawrence pleaded for an alternative. He argued that a simple demonstration of the bomb's powers could persuade Japan to surrender, without any loss of life. Lawrence's words were not heeded. On August 6, 1945, the first atomic bomb was dropped on Hiroshima. On August 9, the second was dropped on Nagasaki.

Ernest Lawrence, the man who had once planned to be a physician so that he could save lives, found himself caught in the spiral of human conflict. Convinced that improved weapons technology could protect the United States from its enemies, Lawrence continued at the forefront of efforts to build increasingly destructive devices. Following the war, he established a weapons-research laboratory in Livermore, California. The experiments carried out in this lab eventually helped bring about the hydrogen bomb. However, Lawrence also joined a U.S. team negotiating with the Soviets for a suspension of nuclear testing in 1958.

Lawrence died unexpectedly of ulcerative colitis on August 27, 1958, in a hospital in Palo Alto, California. His insights into particle acceleration remain with us. His legacy consists of more than the gargantuan new accelerators that crank out millions of times the power of Lawrence's original machine and probe ever further into the secrets of the atom. Nuclear power stations, radiation therapy for cancer patients, carbon dating of materials in archaeology, and, yes, an arsenal of nuclear missiles that could incinerate the globe in a matter of minutes, were all built on knowledge originally uncovered by his invention.

Chronology

August 8, 1901	Ernest Orlando Lawrence born in Canton, South Dakota
1922	earns bachelor's degree from South Dakota State University
1924	earns master's degree from University of Minnesota
1925	earns Ph.D. from Yale; continues on as a Yale faculty member
1928	joins faculty at University of California at Berkeley
1929	conceives idea for cyclotron
January 2, 1931	achieves 80,000 volt acceleration with 4½-inch cyclotron
January 1932	applies for patent on cyclotron
September 1932	first breaks open atoms with cyclotron
1933	creates radioactive carbon 13
1939	is awarded Nobel Prize in physics
1941	produces first uranium 235 for atomic bomb
August 6, 1945	atom bomb is dropped on Hiroshima, Japan
August 9, 1945	atom bomb is dropped on Nagasaki, Japan
August 27, 1958	Lawrence dies at the age of 57

Further Reading

Childs, Herbert. *An American Genius: The Life of Ernest Orlando Lawrence*. New York: Sutton, 1968. A biography of the life of Ernest Lawrence.

Davis, Nuel Pharr. *Lawrence & Oppenheimer*, New York: Da Capo Press, 1986. A lengthy look at two of the dominant physicists of the earlier 20th century. Robert Oppenheimer was the head of the team that developed the first atomic bomb.

Those Inventive Americans. Washington: National Geographic Society, 1971. Very readable for young-adult audiences, it provides a clear understanding of Lawrence's importance.

Wilkes, Daniel. "200 Man-Years of Life," *The Physics Teacher*, September 1965. A straightforward, detailed summary of Lawrence's life and influence.

Chester Carlson
& Xerography

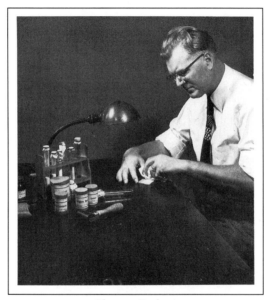

Chester Carlson
(Courtesy of Xerox Corporation)

*C*hester Carlson would probably have been shocked to learn that anyone would be interested in the story of his life. He was constantly frustrated by what he considered to be a dull personality. Carlson was well aware that he did not live life in the fast lane. He had neither the time nor the ability to enjoy the company of friends or to plan fascinating and fun experiences. His idea of a good time was summed up by a sincere statement he made at the age of 22, that "the most pleasure we get from life is sweating." Later in life, when he had amassed an incredible fortune and could afford to do almost anything he wanted, Carlson was asked if there was anything left that he really wanted to do. Carlson's only request: "I would like to die a poor man."

The world seemed to have no place for this lonely inventor, and yet he found his niche. Off by himself in his tiny corner, Chester Carlson started a revolution that was to make an avalanche of information available to the average person. Only 30 years after his invention was perfected, it was difficult to imagine how any office ever functioned without a dry-copy machine.

Chester Floyd Carlson was born in Seattle, Washington, on February 8, 1906, the only child of Olof and Ellen Carlson. Both parents were afflicted with tuberculosis. Olof struggled with the additional burden of arthritis, and the combination of illnesses made it especially difficult for him to earn his living as he did, by working as a barber. Searching for a dry, warm climate that might ease their health problems, the Carlsons moved to the California desert when Chester was three. After a difficult year of living in a tent, they moved to Mexico, where they tried to farm an almost worthless plot of land. Revolution broke out in Mexico when Chester was six, and the family fled to Los Angeles, California, with only one trunkful of belongings. There they lived for a brief time in the home of a doctor for whom Ellen Carlson worked as a housekeeper. This constant uprooting left little time for the shy youngster to develop any friendships.

In 1912 the Carlsons rented a farmhouse near San Bernardino, California. At that time it was a desolate area. There were few families, no friends for Chester, and at times not even a classmate. There was a period when Carlson was the only student at his tiny country school.

Burdened by health problems, the Carlsons, were always scrimping for enough money just to survive. At the age of 12, Chester took on odd jobs such as washing windows to help pay the bills. Olof's health deteriorated steadily until he was confined to his bed, and by the age of 14, Chester was responsible for supporting the family. Instead of dropping out of school, however, Chester simply added more working hours to his schedule, including a job as a sample boy at a cement plant.

Among the other odd jobs that he worked was one at a local print shop. In a deal that was as close as Carlson ever came to splurging on himself, he agreed to accept a small printing press as payment for work that he performed. At that time, Carlson enjoyed chemistry in school and, during what little spare time he had, he printed two issues of a magazine designed for other chemistry buffs.

Having spent so much time by himself, it is not surprising that Carlson developed his own, unique way of looking at things. The story is told of the time when a cousin was visiting the Carlsons in California. The cousin was looking out the window and mentioned that he saw a blackbird out in the yard.

Chester asked him how he knew it was a blackbird. Irritated by such a silly question, the cousin pointed out that it was the size, shape, and color of a blackbird. "But you haven't seen the other side," said Carlson.

Such a way of thinking may have made it awkward for Carlson to mix with other people, but it served him well as an inventor and a tinkerer. While printing his magazine, he began to ask questions about the whole process of getting words onto paper. He started thinking about how the process might be improved, and he began to jot these ideas down into a notebook. There was no telling when an idea might occur to him, though, and so he always carried a loose-leaf notebook in his pocket.

He was 17 when his mother died. That left Chester with the additional task of caring for his ailing father, on top of school and work. He found a more permanent job at the cement plant and, after graduation from high school, made a special arrangement with Riverside Junior College. Beginning in 1925, Carlson was allowed to alternate six weeks of work with six weeks of study.

Carlson was considered something of an overachiever. He put in long hours of study in order to get good grades in his classes. Yet the head of this work-study program, Professor Howard Bliss, recognized that he had special talents. Bliss took a special interest in the student and, for once, Carlson had a friend. Bliss took him on trips, interested him in photography, and helped him to set high goals for himself.

Given the way Carlson agonized over his faults, this raising of his sights may have been Bliss's greatest contribution. Carlson had a difficult time recognizing his own worth. He frequently made lists of his faults and was obsessed with improving himself. This self-conscious attitude, in turn, guaranteed social disaster. Instead of relaxing and being himself with others, Carlson constantly critiqued his performance. He once made a note to himself that he should "call the other fellow crazy once in a while," in hopes that this would make him appear more self-confident.

When his two years with Bliss and Riverside were completed, Carlson attended the California Institute of Technology. There he slipped back into almost total isolation. He lived at home, avoided all contact with campus life, and made no friends. As always, he worked to support himself in addition to his studies. Occasionally, he would find someone to play tennis with. But even in sports his objective was not so much enjoyment as it was keeping up his health.

In his diary he continued to berate himself for his failures. Despite the fact that he was keeping a schedule that would have exhausted most students, he scolded himself for not achieving the detailed objectives he had set.

Meanwhile, he worried about his future. Money had never come easy to the Carlson family. How was he going to earn a living? What career should he choose? In his typical, methodical style he listed his choices. He thought about becoming a poet, a teacher, a businessman, an inventor. Just as typically, he ridiculed his chances. "I have very little indication that I would make a good teacher or inventor," he wrote.

It was while working at a test laboratory in Los Angeles during the summer before his final year at Cal-Tech that he settled on becoming an inventor. But one did not just become an inventor, especially when one was deeply in debt. Carlson decided he could not afford to be choosy about his career. He wrote letters to 82 companies, seeking work. But as the Great Depression settled on the business world, few companies were hiring. Carlson's unspectacular academic record did not help his cause either. Only two companies bothered to respond to Carlson's inquiries and neither of them were interested in him.

When his father died that same year, 1930, Carlson had no reason to stay in California. He moved to New York City, hoping the job prospects were better there. Finally, a position opened up at the Bell Telephone Laboratories. Carlson started out as a research engineer, but he was transferred to the company's patents department in 1931. Two years later, the depression took its toll on the Bell labs and Carlson was let go.

His patent experience enabled him to get a job at a small patent law firm. Within a year he resigned that job to join the patents department of P. R. Mallory and Company, a firm that specialized in electrical components.

Chester Carlson

Carlson's job at Mallory involved preparing documents so that they complied with government regulations. Those regulations required duplicate copies of the patent applications. Although carbon paper was commonly used for typing duplicate copies at the time, it did not work for these documents. Carbon paper was of no help in copying documents that had already been typed. Furthermore, sketches, detailed drawings, and elaborate charts were often important pieces of evidence in a patent claim. Duplication by photography was far too impractical, and that meant that the only way for Carlson to get duplicates was to hand-copy them. This was a tedius process at best. Eye fatigue could also lead to mistakes, especially in someone as near-sighted as Carlson. He was also beginning to experience the arthritis that had crippled his father, and this made copying difficult. He could not help but wonder if there were a better, quicker way to do this.

This need for a duplicating machine rekindled his interest in inventing. Carlson began spending most of his spare time searching the shelves of the New York City Public Library for clues as to how he might make such a machine. He discovered that Eastman-Kodak, the giant photography company, was dabbling in wet-chemical methods of duplication. Carlson instinctively felt that a dry-chemical method of copy would be better. As he searched the technical literature on the subject, he discovered that no one else was studying the practicality of dry-chemical copying. Carlson had a vast field of study all to himself. If he could come up with something that worked, he had a clear path to an important patent.

Carlson became intrigued with the concept of photoconductivity. *Photoconductivity* refers to the effect that light has on the ability of certain materials to conduct electricity. During his search of the technical journals, Carlson discovered an article by Hungarian physicist Paul Selengi. Selengi demonstrated that particles charged by static electricity could be attracted to specific points on a surface.

This was just what Carlson was looking for. Selengi was attracting solid particles in such a way as to form desired shapes. Why couldn't those points on the surface be arranged so that the attracted particles formed letters or even pictures?

Carlson knew immediately that he was on to something important. He set about experimenting with this photoelectric process in the kitchen of his apartment in Queens, New York. As always, he was on a tight budget, but he scrimped and saved enough money to collect the chemicals he needed. Because he could not afford a burner, he used his kitchen stove whenever he needed to apply heat to the process.

Carlson charged metal plates with static electricity, and this caused certain chemical powders to cling to the plate. He began experiments in which he exposed the charged plates to light. Under certain conditions, an intense light could cause portions of the plate to lose their electrostatic charge. When the powder was then sprinkled over the plate, it would would adhere only to those portions of the plate that kept their charge. If only he could get a plate to lose its electrostatic charge in precisely the places needed so that he could form images.

In his early experiments, Carlson used sulfur as a coating for his metal plates. Sulfur is known for its rotten egg smell. The fumes must have made living conditions almost unbearable in his apartment and most unpleasant for his neighbors. A story commonly told of Carlson is that his landlady's daughter came up one evening to complain about the smell he was creating. She became so intrigued with his strange project that the two became friends. In 1934 Chester and Linda were married.

As his experiments progressed, Carlson felt pinched by his lack of income. Most of his colleagues at P. R. Mallory were earning more money than he simply because they held law degrees. The best remedy to that situation, he decided, was to enroll in law school himself. As an added benefit, he would learn how to legally protect his rights to his discovery. By 1936 Carlson was back to his old workaholic habits. Along with his full-time job, he spent his nights studying and his weekends at the library or in his laboratory. His dream moved a step closer to reality when he was awarded his first patent for the basic concept of "electrophotography," as he called it, in October of 1937.

By this time, the Carlsons had put up with a sulfur-filled apartment long enough, and Carlson set up a new laboratory behind his mother-in-law's beauty shop. After years of trying to do everything himself, he hired Otto Kornei, a refugee from Nazi Germany, as an assistant. Money was as tight as ever, however, and the two had to stick to a research budget of $10 a month.

On October 22, 1938, Carlson took a pen and printed the date and the name of the neighborhood in which they were working, "Astoria," on a glass microscope slide. Kornei then rubbed a cotton cloth against a sulfur-coated zinc plate. This charged the plate with static electricity. He then pressed the plate onto the glass slide and held it up to the light. The theory was that the ink should block the light so that the area of the plate beneath the letters would not lose its charge.

Carlson then removed the slide and dusted the plate with a yellowish powder. Next a section of wax paper was pressed to the plate and heated. When Carlson turned over the paper and blew away the excess powder, he saw "10-22-38 Astoria" printed on the wax paper! His patience had been rewarded. At long last things were looking up for Carlson. In 1939 he had a law degree, a valuable patent, and a proven dry-copying process.

If he thought his troubles were behind him, though, he was badly mistaken. For he was still lacking the one thing he most needed—a buyer. In order to make his invention attractive, Carlson saved enough money to pay a model shop to build a prototype in 1939. The model did not work well. While continually improving the process, he tried to peddle the idea to companies such as

In his later years, Carlson looks back at the original prototype of his dry-copying machine.
(Courtesy of Xerox Corporation)

IBM (International Business Machines) and General Electric. His luck with major corporations, however, had not improved since his job-hunting days. With his unpolished, self-conscious manner, he made little impression on busy executives. His machine looked primitive, and his process actually seemed a step backward from both carbon paper and photography. None of the companies could imagine a use for such technology.

After five frustrating years trying to peddle electrophotography, Carlson was out of money and ideas. He was also exhausting the patience of his wife. The only thing that kept him from abandoning the whole project was his stubborn conviction that he had invented something important.

A break finally came when Dr. Russell Dayton, representing a small non-profit research group in Columbus, Ohio, visited the P. R. Mallory offices in 1944. Dayton had come to talk about some other patents. But while visiting with him, Carlson happened to mention his own project. Instead of shrugging him off like so many others had, Dayton actually listened. He took Carlson's ideas back to the Battelle Memorial Institute to ask the opinion of his engineers. They agreed that Carlson might be on to something, and Battelle offered to develop the technology in exchange for a percentage of whatever royalties Carlson would receive.

Carlson was so thrilled that he began spending all his spare time traveling to Columbus. Again, though, his excitement was premature. His wife, tired of having their life controlled by this obsession, divorced him in 1945. Then Battelle decided they could not afford to develop Carlson's copier. This time it was they who went to the big corporations, but they had no better luck than Carlson. The inventor was so strapped financially that he had to borrow money from relatives to keep going.

Fortunately, a small photo-supply manufacturer in Rochester, New York, was becoming nervous about its future. The Haloid Company saw that demand for its products was declining, and it was searching for new products to add to its line. Officials had happened across an article in a technical journal describing Carlson's work. After talking with Carlson and with the Battelle people, Haloid decided to bet its future on this unproven process. In 1946 they began by investing a quarter of their total income in developing Carlson's machine.

First of all, they needed a marketable name for the process, and Carlson's "electrophotography" was too cumbersome. An Ohio State professor suggested the name *xerography* from two Greek words meaning "dry writing." Inspired by the success of cross-town rival Kodak, whose name began and ended with the same letter, Haloid decided to call their first copy machine a XeroX.

Carlson eagerly worked with the Haloid engineers to make improvements. He and his second wife, Dorris, whom he married in 1946, eventually moved to suburban Rochester to be near the company. But, as usual, he was not a ready mixer with his new colleagues. He was so protective of his ideas that, for a long time, he refused to mix his copy chemicals in the Haloid lab. He preferred to concoct the formula in his own basement and then bring it with him. Eventually, he loosened up, and others began to consider him an easy person to work with.

Haloid made a number of changes in the process. One of these was the replacement of foul-smelling sulfur with a more effective material, selenium. In 1948, 10 years to the day after Carlson's first successful experiment, Haloid and Battelle unveiled their plans at an Optical Society Convention in Detroit, Michigan.

A year later, Haloid introduced its first copier, the XeroX Model A. Once again, however, Carlson had to put the cork back in his champagne bottle. The clumsy-looking model was privately dubbed the "ox-box." Not only was it unsightly, but it required 14 different steps, each of which had to be followed exactly. Making a single copy seemed nearly as time-consuming and laborious as photography. Customers saw little advantage in this dry-copy product, and they ignored it.

As years went by, Carlson began to wonder if he would ever make any money from his invention. His exclusive patents were beginning to run out before they had realized any profit.

In 1955, Haloid came out with a completely automatic copier that used a drum instead of a flat plate. This model was simple enough to attract some buyers. In 1959 Haloid Xerox collected $32 million in sales. But it was not until 1960 that Xerox copy machines really caught on. The company came out with a machine that could produce clear, fast copies with the push of a button. The Xerox 914 (named because of the size of paper it used, 9" × 14") became one of the most successful products ever introduced. In 1966, the company, which had changed its name to Xerox, topped $500 million a year in sales. Two years later, sales climbed to more than a billion dollars. By 1984 Xerox had become one of the United States' top 50 exporters.

As Carlson had envisioned, document copying has made it possible for vast amounts of information to be distributed among

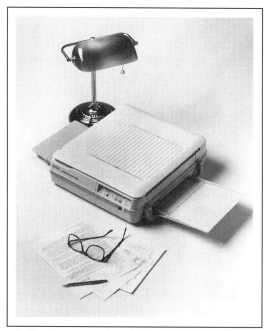

*Carlson's process has been refined to the point
where Xerox can package the whole system in a
desktop Personal Copier.*
(Courtesy of Xerox Corporation)

great numbers of people. Copy machines have made it possible for business to be contracted much more quickly and efficiently than ever before.

Now the very corporations that could see no use for Carlson's dry-copy machine would be hard-pressed to do without them. Today one can hardly go into an office, a library, or even a post office without seeing a copy machine. By the end of 1987, there were more than five million copy machines in the United States alone, pumping out nearly 500 billion copies a year. Dry copying had become so easy and so universal that new laws had to be drawn up governing the use of copy machines in duplicating copyrighted material.

Following the success of the 914, Carlson became rich beyond his wildest fantasies. One might expect that the shock of fabulous wealth after so many years of poverty might have gone to his head. But Carlson remained immune to the pleasures of society that so many people crave. Consistent to the end, he very deliberately drew up lists of places and causes to which he should give money. Ever uncomfortable in society's spotlight, he insisted on giving his gifts anonymously. It is estimated that he gave away more than $100 million.

On September 19, 1968, Carlson finished a conference early in the day. To fill time before he was to meet his wife, he went alone to a movie theater. It was there that an usher later found him dead of a heart attack.

Carlson died as he had lived most of his life, off in his own corner, alone and unnoticed. It is one of the ironies of the 20th century that a man who had so little contact with his society could play such a huge role in shaping the future of that society.

Chronology

February 8, 1906	Chester Floyd Carlson born in Seattle, Washington
1920	takes over as main support of family
1930	receives physics degree from California Institute of Technology, moves to New York City, finds work with Bell Telephone Labs
1933	is laid off by Bell, eventually joined patent department of P. R. Mallory and Company
1937	gains first patent for concept of electrophotography
October 22, 1938	first successful demonstration of electrophotography
1939	builds prototype dry copier
1944	gains backing of Battelle Memorial Institute
1946	Haloid Company risks major investment on Carlson's invention
1949	XeroX Model A copier is marketed
1955	Xerox develops fully automatic copier
1960	Xerox 914 copier is introduced, becomes huge success
September 19, 1968	Carlson died at age 62

Further Reading

Golembeski, Dean J. "Struggling to Become an Inventor," *Invention & Technology*, Winter 1989. This article, written by a man who currently works for Xerox, is the most complete source of information available on Chester Carlson.

Jacobson, Gary. *American Samurai*. New York: Macmillan, 1986. Along with telling the story of the emergence of Xerox as an international corporation, the book provides some interesting personal glimpses of Carlson.

Howard Aiken
& the Computer

Howard Hathaway Aiken
(Division of Applied Sciences, Harvard
University—photographed by Paul
Donaldson)

---

*T*he temptation to stereotype inventors can be cured very easily by comparing Chester Carlson to Howard Aiken. In contrast to the shy, stocky, mild-mannered loner who quietly developed the copy machine, Aiken was a tall, impeccably groomed man, a natural leader who could be so demanding and combative that he provoked a decade-long feud with the president of IBM (International Business Machines).

"I am a simple man and I want simple answers!" he often roared at his associates, and many a table was rattled by the pounding of his fists. Unlike Carlson, the secretive patent expert, Aiken spurned the whole idea of patenting and freely shared his ideas with hundreds of visitors from halfway around the world. His only interests were in getting the most out of people and in getting the job done.

Because of his disdain for patents and because most of the actual machinery that he used was designed by his IBM associates, Aiken is not often included among the ranks of influential inventors. But it was Aiken's ideas and his forceful leadership that brought about the invention of one of the most sweeping innovations of our time. Aiken was the first to demonstrate that a powerful, automatic digital calculator could be built. Once that breakthrough was made, others recognized the potential of such machines. From Aiken's takeoff point, computer technology has exploded to where machines now routinely crank out answers that humans could not begin to calculate in a million years.

Howard Hathaway Aiken was born in Hoboken, New Jersey, on March 8, 1900, and grew up in Indianapolis, Indiana. Aiken's life contains two similarities to Chester Carlson's. One is the bond shared by almost all notable 20th-century inventors—their work took priority over their social life. Aiken did not marry until the age of 43 and, like Carlson, he was married twice.

The more striking similarity with Chester Carlson is the manner in which both got through high school. Family finances forced Aiken to begin working nights as a switchboard attendant for a local power company following the eighth grade. Like Carlson, he benefited from a flexible school system. Aiken's superintendent at Arsenal Technical High School allowed him to take correspondence courses so that he could finish the necessary high school work without having to quit his job.

Aiken then found employment with the Madison Gas and Electric Company that supported him while he worked at the University of Wisconsin in Madison, Wisconsin. Immediately after Aiken earned his bachelor's degree in 1923, Madison Gas and Electric rewarded him with a position as an electrical engineer. His area of expertise was in designing and reconstructing electrical generating stations. After working on similar projects for Westinghouse Electric and the Line Material Company, he became restless for new challenges.

In 1931, Aiken began studying physics at the University of Chicago, and eventually he transferred to Harvard University in Cambridge, Massachusetts. While working on his masters and doctorate degrees at Harvard, he delved into research on the properties of vacuum tubes. He found that a proper analysis of some of their properties depended on complex equations. Aiken spent countless hours grinding away at these long and tedious calculations. Some of the equations that he hoped to use in his work proved to be so mind-boggling that no human could possibly perform all the calculations required.

Aiken began to wonder if some kind of automatic calculating machine could be built to solve these time-consuming problems. For nearly two years he kept most of these thoughts to himself until he could determine whether there was any chance of building such a device.

He looked into the history of tabulating machines and discovered that an Englishman named Charles Babbage had actually come fairly close more than a century ago. Babbage had not had the money or the backing to complete his task, nor had he had the advantage of such things as electrical circuits and machine tools that could have easily solved many of his problems. Yet his "analytical engine" provided some novel ideas on how such a machine could be made to work. Babbage had divided his machine into two parts: a "store" that held the numbers to be calculated, and a "mill" that actually performed the work on those numbers. The machine was controlled by punchcards that gave logical, step-by-step directions to the machine.

After pondering the need for a device that could calculate, Aiken wrote a memo in 1937 called "Proposed Automatic Calculating Machine." In it he noted that there were some machines on the market that could do some simple tabulating and sorting with the use of punch cards. But the sciences, he noted, had advanced into areas of study that were far beyond the abilities of these crude, human-operated instruments. Some physics equations were so complicated that several lines across a printed page were required just to write them.

Aiken then outlined the design and construction of a machine that could be used to solve virtually any mathematical problem, no matter how difficult. He proposed a machine that was fully automatic from the first input to the final result and that could perform its functions rapidly with guaranteed, error-free results.

The proposal was so outlandishly ambitious that Aiken found little support at first. He was told by his Harvard mentors that he would never amount to much in the academic world if he insisted in chasing such unlikely dreams. When he tried to present his ideas to companies that sold desktop calculators, the reception was no warmer. While some of them conceded that Aiken had an intriguing idea, none thought it practical enough to commit any money to it.

At last Professor Theodore Brown of the Harvard Business School suggested to him that IBM might be interested in developing his ideas. At the time, IBM was a small company that had made a number of innovations in punch-card operated business machines.

IBM president Thomas Watson immediately liked Aiken's concept, as well as the idea of associating his small business with the prestigious Harvard University. J. W. Bryce, an IBM inventor with more than 400 improvements in the design of calculating-machine parts to his credit, was brought in for consultation. When Bryce expressed enthusiasm for the project, IBM offered to provide both the funding and the expertise. A team of engineers, led by C. D. Lake, was assigned to assist Aiken in his research. It was a unique adventure in high-technology in that neither Aiken nor IBM expected any direct financial gain from the project. Aiken was interested only in getting the machine built, while IBM hoped to gain prestige by its involvement with Harvard.

The early days of the project consisted largely of conversations between Aiken and the IBM engineers. Aiken would spell out exactly how the machine was to operate, and the engineers would tell him what equipment was available that could meet his specifications. Eventually, they shaped a plan for putting together the Automatic Sequence Controlled Calculator (ASCC). Such an enormous undertaking demanded the highest standards of excellence and integrity. Aiken, with his passion for pure research and his disinterest in patents, was able to set and maintain these standards throughout the project. Colleagues also credited him with an uncanny ability to discover the easiest solution to a problem.

While this work was going on, Aiken received his Ph.D. in 1939 and, two years later, was inducted into the United States Naval Reserve. This World War II military duty did not disrupt his work on the ASCC because the navy had become keenly interested in the machine. Commander Aiken was assigned to stay at Harvard and continue directing the computer research.

Aiken was described by those who knew him as a "driven man." It was later said of him that his main hobby was work and that the only time he ever relaxed was during rides to and from airports. He expected others to be just as intense about their work. There were times when he pushed his associates into working 24 hours a day on his project. He frequently challenged them with assignments that seemed impossible, and then urged them to "have fun" carrying out the task. Few days went by without Aiken peering over the shoulder of someone working on the ASCC and asking, "Are you making any numbers?" Although he did not demand perfection from his workers, he did expect them to learn from their errors. Anyone who made the same mistake twice could expect to hear about it.

Aiken's gruff manner and explosive temper could intimidate both friends and enemies. Grace Hopper, who became one of the world's most respected computer programmers, recalls Aiken's first words to her. Upon reporting for duty on the ASCC project, she was greeted by Aiken, who demanded to know what had taken her so long. When some Harvard faculty members sought to maintain some supervision over the IBM project, Aiken so totally disrupted their meeting that they made no more attempts to bother him. One colleague once claimed that the trick to working with Aiken was to match him shout for shout and to answer his table-thumping with some pounding of one's own.

Despite the stormy atmosphere Aiken created, his students and staff held him in profound respect. Even when their leader was not around to push them, his computer team showed incredible devotion to their tasks. Once, they were deeply involved in some aspect of the project when a hurricane struck the nearby coast. Aiken's team kept working while the winds and rain began to rage around them. By the time they finished their task, the storm was in full force. The team linked themselves together in a human chain and staggered from tree to tree to make their way back to their quarters.

Aiken also had a gift for guiding and inspiring people to accomplish things that they never knew they could. Grace Hopper was stunned one day when, without warning, Aiken told her to write a book. When she protested that she didn't know anything about writing, Aiken simply responded that she was in the navy now. Hopper accepted the challenge and produced one of the most influential books in computer history, a manual for the operation of the ASCC.

Aiken's Mark I
(Courtesy of IBM Corporation)

It took until January of 1943 before Aiken's machine was ready for its first test. The Mark I, as it was called, correctly solved the problem given to it. At the end of that year, Harvard faculty members were summoned to the IBM facilities for a demonstration. After more than five years of work and a quarter million dollars of IBM's money, Aiken's dream had been achieved. In February of 1944, IBM engineers took apart the machine and shipped it to Harvard, where it was reassembled in an air-conditioned basement.

Aiken managed to create considerable tension even at the crowning moment of his project. Normally the commander was most generous in acknowledging the efforts of others and in deflecting credit from himself. But for some reason, when speaking at a dedication ceremony for the Mark I in 1945, he failed to mention the crucial contributions of IBM. IBM president Thomas Watson, Sr., who had just donated the machine to Harvard University, was livid. Another of Aiken's shouting matches ensued. The result was that, for more than a decade afterward, the very mention of Aiken's name would provoke dark curses at IBM headquarters.

The Mark I was the world's first completely automatic computer. It was built to monstrous proportions, as it had to be in order to house all the equipment that Aiken needed for his "super-brain." It was 51 feet long and 8 feet high. It contained 530 miles of wire, more than 1,200 ball bearings, 175,000 electrical connections, and roughly 750,000 parts.

The design of the Mark I was patterned after a switchboard that Aiken remembered from his days as a switchboard operator. The left-hand side of the machine held 1,440 dials. These gave the computer the numbers that it would be working with. Operations on those numbers were performed by 72 counters or registers, devices that could store numbers as well as manipulate them. Numbers were moved from one place to another in the machine in the form of electrical impulses.

These registers needed to be given instructions so that they knew what to do with the numbers that were dialed in. Ribbons or cards were punched with a pattern of holes according to a codebook that Aiken had designed. These ribbons were fed into four slots in the machine that contained sensitive mechanisms. Tiny brushes within these mechanisms felt the holes and responded by telegraphing the orders to the proper places. The registers would take the orders in sequence, completing the required computation before moving on to the next instruction. The 72 registers could also communicate with each other through electrical signals. In addition, the Mark I contained spools of ribbons that carried mathematical tables for use in solving more complex problems. All results were printed out on two electric typewriters positioned at the far right of the machine.

Despite its bulk and its dazzling array of components, the Mark I was driven by a four-horsepower motor that used no more electricity than the average washing machine. Repairs could be accomplished without sophisticated equipment. Whenever a relay was suspected of failing, the operators merely turned out the lights, went behind the front panel and used a purse-sized mirror to help locate the telltale sparks given off by a faulty component.

"Bessie," as the Mark I was affectionately called by its operators, could perform three additions per second. It required about 15 seconds to work out a complicated division problem and as much as a minute to compute a trigonometry problem. The machine was far more precise than was required for most problems—it could give an answer to 23 significant digits.

Many scientists and businesspeople had trouble envisioning much use for this new invention. Aiken, himself, saw his ASCC as a one-of-a-kind machine when he first proposed it. There did not seem to be very many enormously complex problems that would require the speed and precision of the computer, and it was far too expensive and cumbersome to build them just for convenience' sake.

But by the time that the Mark I was finished, the demand for computers had grown far beyond its capacity. The armed forces, for example, were developing a new generation of long-range artillery. In order to be effective, angles of trajectory needed to be calculated with far greater precision than before. During the last months of World War II, the U.S. Navy was feeding problems to the Mark I 24 hours a day. Rather than solving all the tough problems, computers were opening the door to ever more complex problems.

The navy asked Aiken to build another one of these machines for their use. The second of Aiken's computers, the Mark II, was completed in 1947, by which time Aiken had completed his active duty with the navy. The Mark II was similar to the earlier version, in that it relied on mechanical switches rather than electrical switches. The Mark II was able to solve problems more than twice as quickly as the Mark I. While aware that electrical components would allow machines to make calculations far more rapidly than this, Aiken was more concerned about reliability.

Mark II was also involved in coining the term *debugging*. During the summer of 1945, the machine malfunctioned. Workers discovered that the problem was a moth that had flown into the apparatus, where it had been killed. When Aiken walked into the room, asking why no one was making any numbers, he was told that they were "debugging" the computer. The phrase is now commonly used for a procedure that removes flaws from computer programs.

By the mid-1940s, the potential of computers had become obvious and many others began to experiment with their own designs. After noting the success of other computer designers with electricity, Aiken converted to an electrical design for his Mark III, also a navy project. Completed in 1949, it had about the same

*Aiken inspects a nest of cable interconnections
in his Mark II.*
(National Archives)

capacity as a modern personal computer. At first Aiken's crew had trouble getting the machine to work consistently. Eventually the problem was traced to the effects of heating and cooling on the machine. The simple solution was to leave the machine on all the time, after which it worked reliably. The Mark III introduced such innovations as magnetic-tape drives, but it was still cumbersome, requiring 5,000 vacuum tubes and 2,000 mechanical relays. Aiken then made one more series of refinements with his Mark IV, which he built for the air force.

By the time he was working on Mark IV, scientists throughout the world had come to realize that Aiken's invention was far more than just a mathematical toy. By the beginning of 1951, there were 11 large-scale computers in operation in the United States. Five European countries had developed their own giant calculators, and several others were working on it. Aiken freely shared his knowledge with whomever was interested. By 1951 he had welcomed more than 500 Europeans who had come for brief visits, and he had worked with more than two dozen who had stayed for longer periods of time.

Aiken's original computers made an immediate impact on the world, beyond the aiming of navy guns. As Wilbur Wright had discovered many years before, there were major errors in mathematical tables that had been commonly accepted for decades. Aiken's machines were able to discover a large number of these errors within the first few years of operation.

But it was not the actual work done by the Mark I or any of Aiken's improved versions that has earned Aiken a revered spot in the history of technology. In fact, his computers were scarcely in operation before they became obsolete. The larger impact of Howard Aiken was the impetus he gave to the entire field of computer science. *Popular Mechanics* magazine was one of the first to recognize the impact that Aiken's dream would have on the world. An article published in October of 1944 says of the ASCC, "it will accelerate the exploration of nearly every field of knowledge. This Paul Bunyan will stride through forests of figures that might not otherwise be explored for centuries if they were ever explored at all."

That has certainly proved to be the case. The tremendous speed and efficiency of computers has created a wealth of knowledge far beyond what the unaided human brain could ever accomplish. Modern supercomputers can perform at a sustained rate of more than a billion calculations per second. Such speeds have multiplied the amount of knowledge available to humans in virtually every area of study. Computers can sort through thousands of variables and provide the precise information desired. They can calculate and regulate the adjustments necessary to steer unmanned spacecraft thousands of miles into space. The use of computers in CT scans have made it possible for doctors to see inside the human skull. Computers can handle the millions of bits of information necessary to simulate the effects of complex systems. They have increased our ability to predict weather, to calculate the effects of pollution, and store information. Computers have improved everything from the accuracy of weapons and stability of airplanes to the reliability of engineering, the efficiency of word processing, and dependability of scientific instruments.

Aiken kept up with the rapid advances in computer technology throughout most of his life. Many of the brightest minds in computers were steered into the field under his guidance. He coauthored and edited a 24-volume series of technical works on computers before retiring as a professor at Harvard in 1962. From there he went on to found his own company, Howard Aiken Industries, specializing in communications and electronics technology.

Throughout his life, he never tired of reminding people that computers such as he designed were only servants. They would never replace human thought. Their only advantage was that they could take the work that humans gave them and do it more quickly and painlessly.

At the same time, he was well aware that computers had, in some areas, surpassed the power of the human brain by many orders of magnitude, and he was aware of how drastically this new power could alter human society. At a retirement dinner in 1962, he reflected on the technology that he had pioneered. "I hope to God that this will be used for the benefit of mankind and not it's detriment," he said.

Aiken died in his sleep at his home in Fort Lauderdale, Florida, on March, 15, 1973. A colleague once said of him, "Howard dreams up the most fantastic things, and then gets them done." There is probably no more fitting tribute that can be given to an inventor in this or any age.

Chronology

March 8, 1900	Howard Hathaway Aiken born in Indianapolis, Indiana
1923	obtains engineering degree from University of Wisconsin, is employed as an electrical engineer by Madison Gas & Electric
1931	enrolls at University of Chicago to study physics
1937	prepares memo outlining his plan for an automatic calculating machine, gains cooperation of IBM
1939	receives Ph.D. from Harvard
1941	joins United States Naval Reserve
1943	Automatic Sequence Controlled Calculator (Mark I) is successfully tested
1944	Mark I is installed at Harvard
1947	Mark II is completed
1949	Mark III, Aiken's first electronic calculator, is completed
1962	Aiken retires from teaching at Harvard
March 15, 1973	dies at the age of 73

Further Reading

Billings, Charlene W. *Grace Hopper: Navy Admiral and Computer Pioneer*. Hillside, N.J.: Enslow, 1989. Written for younger readers, this story of computer expert Grace Hopper includes anecdotes about Hopper's boss, Howard Aiken.

Ritchie, David. *The Computer Pioneers*. New York: Simon & Schuster, 1986. This book briefly describes the contributions of many innovators who contributed to modern computer technology, and includes a good deal of information on Aiken.

William Shockley
& the Transistor

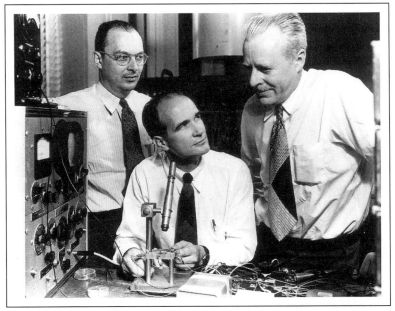

John Bardeen, William Shockley, and Walter Brattain (shown left to right) demonstrate one of the procedures that led them to the invention of the transistor in 1948.
(AT&T Bell Labs)

*I*n 1955, William Shockley migrated back to the land of his youth, to a valley along the southern fringe of San Francisco, California. This was the place where, as a child, he had performed magic shows for his family and neighbors. Now he was preparing to produce a magic show the likes of which the world had never seen. Surrounding himself with a dozen or so of the nation's best-trained physicists and chemists, he began cultivating an entirely new business.

His enterprise was based on a device that he and his associates at the Bell Telephone Laboratories in New Jersey had recently invented. By all appearances, it was nothing more than an odd piece of hardware, a small chunk of material with a few wires attached. Its main ingredient was silicon, better known to most of us as ordinary sand. By itself it could perform no impressive feats. One of its main functions, in fact, was to perform the mundane task of turning switches on and off.

Shockley's business was not able to get a spectacular yield from this strange invention. But some of his associates continued the magic show. Before long the seed that Shockley brought produced a bumper crop of high-technology. Within two decades the valley was so overrun with electronics wizardry based on Shockley's device that it was dubbed Silicon Valley.

The seed that Shockley had planted in Silicon Valley was the transistor, and the offshoots of this invention have carried Howard Aiken's goal of accelerating human knowledge far beyond anything Aiken could have dreamed. Companies are now cranking out thousands of microscopic flecks of material, each of which is crammed with more information-storing capacity than the most powerful computer that Howard Aiken ever built!

The word most commonly used to describe the leader of the team that invented the transistor is *genius*. William Shockley was a brilliant, hard-driving man with a passion for science and a fierce hatred of mediocrity. That relentless pursuit of excellence was a two-edged sword. It helped bring about the discovery of what *Newsweek* called "probably the most important invention in electronics in 40 years." At the same time, it led Shockley into some bizarre theories that embarrassed the scientific community and cast a shadow over the waning days of his career.

William Bradford Shockley was born on February 13, 1910, in London, England, where his parents were attending to business. The family returned to their home in Palo Alto, California, when he was three.

William Shockley was an only child, the son of highly educated parents. His father, William, was a mining engineer, and his mother, May, a federal surveyor of mineral lands during the Nevada gold rush.

Shockley's aversion to being average was fostered by his parents, who kept him out of school until age eight because they thought he could learn more at home. When he finally did attend school, he did not care much for the experience.

His interest in academics was kindled outside of the classroom, at the home of a neighbor. The neighbor, who taught physics at Stanford University, showed unusual patience with children. He explained various scientific concepts so that William could understand them and showed him how a radio works.

Shockley became intrigued with this new world of science, and his parents encouraged his interest. His father enjoyed discussing science problems with him, while his mother helped him dig into the world of mathematics. William soon discovered he was far better at science than the others in his class, and his competitive drive pushed him to stay on top. Like many inventors, he stoked his interest in innovative technology by reading science fiction.

After spending two years at Palo Alto Military Academy, Shockley attended Hollywood High School and graduated from there at the age of 17. He then spent one year at UCLA before moving on to the California Institute of Technology in Pasadena. Coincidentally, he was at Cal-Tech at the same time as Chester Carlson. Shockley received his undergraduate degree from Cal-Tech in 1932. He then received a teaching fellowship from the Massachusetts Institute of Technology (MIT), where he studied the structure of crystals for his graduate work.

The Ph.D. he earned from MIT in 1936 helped him attract job offers from a number of large companies. Shockley chose to work for the Bell Telephone Company in their new research laboratory in Murray Hill, New Jersey. Many 20th-century engineers and scientists began by working on Lee De Forest's vacuum tubes, and Shockley was no exception. His first assignment for Bell was work on a special type of vacuum tube that could act as an amplifier. An amplifier is a device that can transform a weak electrical current into a stronger one.

Shockley's research in this area was not successful. But he was not one to be daunted by failure. In fact, like Goddard, who spoke of "negative information," Shockley once declared "creative failure" to be one of the keys to invention. He believed that a good inventor learned as much from mistakes as from successes. While working on the vacuum tube project, he listened as one of his supervisors described a vision for the Bell Telephone Company. The growing number of telephone subscribers was beginning to overwhelm the company's mechanical switchboard method of operation. This executive hoped that Bell researchers could take the pressure off their equipment by designing an electronic system that would connect all the circuits automatically.

Shockley knew that vacuum tubes, which were currently the most workable means of controlling electrons, could accomplish this. But vacuum tubes were hardly ideal for the large-scale electronic functions that they were asked to perform. They worked by boiling off electrons from a heated filament. This required a great deal of space and consumed large amounts of energy. Vacuum tubes were fragile—they broke easily and gave off so much heat that they frequently burned out.

Since there did not seem to be any way of overcoming these deficiencies, Shockley pondered alternative ways to move electrons. His investigations led him to focus on a curious group of materials called semiconductors. In electrical terms, semiconductors fall somewhere between conductors and insulators. Conductors, such as copper, conduct electricity easily. Insulators, such as rubber, do not conduct electricity. Semiconductors are capable of conducting a limited amount of electricity.

Semiconductors had been used by electrical engineers since the days of the early crystal radios. It had recently been discovered that semiconductors could be used to detect radar waves. Vacuum tubes could also be used for that purpose. Shockley reasoned that if semiconductors could duplicate one of the functions of a vacuum tube, they might be able to duplicate others.

The problem was that no one understood how semiconductors worked. It made no sense to physicists that a single material could both conduct and insulate. About all that could be said to explain the behavior of semiconductors was that there were "holes" in semiconductor material through which electrons could pass easily. Shockley was just beginning to put together some ideas on the subject of semiconductors when his work was interrupted by World War II. Shockley put aside his physics and spent the years from 1940 to 1945 evaluating weapons systems for the United States armed forces.

When the war ended, Shockley returned to Bell to continue his work. Bell executives made a courageous decision to pursue work in semiconductors. Without any clear idea of what useful products, if any, would come from semiconductor research, they invested millions of dollars in research. Shockley was appointed to a large team of workers that also included long-time Bell scientist Walter Brattain and newcomer John Bardeen.

Brattain was the man who performed most of the actual experiments for the group. Bardeen's role was to analyze and explain the results that Brattain was getting. Shockley was the project leader. His job was to provide the direction and the inspiration for the rest. Those who worked with him on the semiconductor research have always confessed to being in awe of his talents in this regard.

As with the others in this book, Shockley was almost totally immersed in his research. The world of scientific discovery was so enjoyable for him that he rarely felt any need for outside recreation. Shockley's curiosity attracted him to all kinds of problems and, as a result, work and play were very nearly the same thing for him. He spent as much time working on research at home as he did at the office. When he did break away to exercise in some kind of sport, he continued to act like a scientist. Mountain climbing was treated as another series of problems to solve. Sailing posed the challenge of making his craft faster and more stable than other boats.

As the project got under way, Shockley proposed that they examine the effect of an electrical field on semiconductors. According to his calculations, an external electric field should influence the ability of the semiconductor to carry electrons. One kind of current, for instance a negatively charged one, might be able to increase the flow of electrons through a semiconductor. It stood to reason, then, that by switching to the opposite current (positive in this case), one could decrease the flow of electrons. Shockley hoped this ability to turn on and off the electric flow might be the key to the "electric circuit switch" that Bell was looking for.

When Brattain performed the experiments, he could not find that the electric field was making any difference at all. Puzzled, Shockley asked Bardeen to check his calculations. Bardeen agreed that, according to all existing theories, the electric field should have made a difference. Apparently semiconductors were more complicated than anyone had realized. It was time for the creative failure that Shockley liked to talk about. Rather than harbor the disappointment of their failed experiment, the team treated it as a new challenge. Perhaps if they could find out why the field effect was not working then they might learn something useful about semiconductors.

It was Bardeen who suggested that the unknown factor that was disturbing everything must be surface interference. For some reason the current was unable to penetrate past the surface of the semiconductor. Bardeen and Brattain tried to get past this barrier by running the electric current into the semiconductor through a conducting liquid.

This proved moderately successful, and the team kept searching for more effective ways of breaking through the surface interference. They discovered that good results could be achieved by placing two wire "contact points" close together on a piece of germanium, which is a semiconductor commonly found in zinc ore. A current passed through one of these contacts could break through the surface interference and conduct electricity to a metal plate on the other side of the germanium.

Brattain's experiments showed that something quite unexpected was also occurring. A weak current flowing through the semiconductor from one contact point to the metal base on the other side created a "hole" in the semiconductor. In other words, it changed a small area of the semiconductor into a very good conductor. This allowed the second contact point to send a much stronger current through to the metal base. This phenomenon was called transfer of resistance. It provided engineers with a way to boost, or amplify, a weak current to many times its original strength.

Most of this new ground in semiconductor knowledge was broken within two months, November and December of 1947. When Shockley's group reported their results, the Bell supervisors knew that they had come across something significant. They spent six months sorting out the patent requirements and preparing for their stunning announcement. A competition was held at Bell Laboratories to name this new device. The name *transistor*, a shortened form of *transfer resistor* was suggested by Dr. John Pierce, and this was the chosen name.

On June 30, 1948, Bell Telephone officials broke the news to the world. The reaction of the press was the media version of a stifled yawn. Bell spokespeople tried to explain the significance of the device: that it was an electronic valve for controlling the flow of electrons, that it could do nearly everything that the vacuum tube could do for a fraction of the cost. But it was difficult for most people to understand what was so earth-shattering about an electronic valve, especially when it turned out to be nothing more than a tiny, 1/16-inch-thick chunk of matter with a few wires sticking out of it. The carefully staged unveiling received scant mention in papers around the country.

As it turned out, Bill Shockley had made the point contact transistor obsolete by the time of the news conference. Immediately after the transistor was developed, Shockley set out to make a detailed analysis of *why* it worked. Within one month of the first laboratory success with the transistor, his research helped him to work out a plan for a new, improved transistor.

The point contact transistor proved to be unreliable because of the delicate nature of the contact points. Shockley's design eliminated the need for those thin, soldered wires that could so easily be jarred loose. Instead of running contacts from one side of the semiconductor to a metal base on the other side, he put the metal base in the middle. This base was sandwiched by two layers of semiconductor that contained the contact points.

It took until 1950 before lab technicians could make this design work and into the next year before it was introduced to the public. But it was this junction design that became the industry standard.

Only when the transistor was turned into consumer products did most people realize what a marvelous device it was. Three of the most visible products—hearing aids, portable radios, and microphones—made use of the device's ability to amplify weak signals. Almost unnoticed by the public was the revolution created by the transistors ability to switch current on and off.

At the time that the transistor came along, computer technology had nearly reached a dead end. Improvements in the memory and processing speed of computers could be made only by adding more vacuum tubes. The largest computers were already burning out vacuum tubes almost as fast as technicians could replace them.

Using transistors in place of vacuum tubes pulled computer designers out of their rut. Transistors were tiny, produced no heat, and did not burn out, so there was almost no limit to how many one could use in a machine. Because they used only a tiny fraction of the power of vacuum tubes, transistors made computers far more affordable. Computers using transistors could process numbers more quickly than the old computers because their transistors required no warm-up time and because they eliminated the hundreds of miles of wiring through which current in vacuum tube computers had to travel.

In the mid-1950s, Shockley decided to ride the crest of his own scientific breakthrough. He left the Bell labs and headed back to the Palo Alto area to set up Shockley Semiconductor. While he was organizing this venture, word came that Shockley and his associates Bardeen and Brattain had been chosen as the Nobel Prize winners in physics for 1956. Typical of his analytical, probing mind, Shockley performed a thorough analysis of the previous Nobel Prize acceptance speeches in preparing for his own.

Shockley's continued investigations into semiconductors led to more than 80 patents. His Shockley Semiconductor could also be considered a success in that its owner was able to profit from its sale a few years later. His enthusiasm for pursuing new mysteries never waned, nor did his energy. When a serious automobile accident in 1971 hospitalized him, Shockley refused to slow down. With his commanding presence he was able to get hospital personnel to set up an office in his hospital room.

But, as one colleague put it, Shockley was "too far ahead of his time" to develop a practical semiconductor product from his theories. It was left to some of the researchers he brought out west with him to capitalize on the miniaturization revolution that he had started.

In 1959, Robert Noyce of Fairchild Semiconductor and Jack Kilby of Texas Instruments modified Shockley's junction transistor into an even smaller, simpler device—the computer chip. This innovation made it possible for many more electronic components to be stored on microscopic pieces of semiconductor (usually silicon). By the early 1980s a $\frac{1}{4}$-inch microchip could hold 10 times the electrical components of the 30-ton ENIAC, the first all-electric computer ever built, and could function at $\frac{1}{30,000}$ the cost of the ENIAC.

While William Shockley's transistor gained ever more respect in the world, however, it's inventor fell from public favor. There were those who complained that Shockley's enormous talent for scientific research was being wasted as he became preoccupied with business concerns. An even larger waste was the effort Shockley began to put into his social theories. In his intense drive for excellence and his hatred of mediocrity, he came to view his own success as a model of what society should be cultivating. From there it was a short step into believing himself to be a model of what a human should be.

Shockley gave much of the credit for his success to the genes he inherited from his parents. His views on improving the lot of humankind through genetics grew more and more radical to the point where he participated in a sperm bank where the sperm of

Nobel Prize winners could be used by infertile couples to pass on "superior" genetic traits. He also declared that blacks were genetically inferior to whites. Shockley's statements stunned and angered the scientific world. By the time of his death on August 12, 1989, he had lost much of the respect he had built up over his career.

Despite his repugnant views, William Shockley was certainly one of the most influential people who ever lived. The effects of his invention on the world have been beyond calculating. The miniaturization of electronic components created by the transistor has made millions of times more information available to us than ever before. By operating on roughly one-millionth the power required by a vacuum tube, the transistor gave computer operators, in effect, a million times more power to work with.

United States society has been so changed by the transistor that it can no longer function without it. Government data and communications, financial transactions, business records, scientific

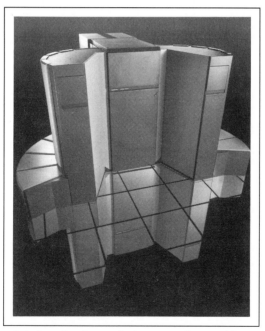

Miniaturization techniques made possible a new generation of supercomputers, including this CRAY Y-MP/832 model that contains 32 million 64-bit words of memory.
(Courtesy of Cray Research, Inc.)

literature, and all the other functions of computers described in the previous chapter depend on the ability of transistors to switch on and off. Pocket calculators built with microchips have become the standard means for processing numbers. Industrial production has been boosted by transistorized robots who take over menial jobs of welding, inspection, and assembly once performed by humans. Satellites beam back data to earth, thanks to the transistor.

Wherever electricity is used to serve humankind, transistors have so increased its production that it seems like magic. In this world of transistors and computer chips, one invention feeds another invention so rapidly that the world changes before our eyes. Microchip technology is moving ahead so quickly that products are almost obsolete from the moment they are introduced. The magic show that William Shockley began goes on. There is no telling when, if ever, it will finally end.

Chronology

February 13, 1910	William Bradford Shockley born in London, England
1913	family moves back to Palo Alto, California
1932	receives degree from Cal-Tech
1936	receives Ph.D. from MIT; joins Bell Telephone Laboratories and begins research on semiconductors
1940–45	evaluates weapons systems for United States armed forces
December 1947	team of Shockley, Brattain, and Bardeen invents the transistor
June 1948	Bell announces the transistor invention; Shockley improves the transistor with his junction version
1955	Shockley relocates to California
1956	Shockley, Brattain, and Bardeen are awarded Nobel Prize in physics
1959	Noyce designs the computer chip
August 12, 1989	Shockley dies at age 79

Further Reading

Aaseng, Nathan. *The Inventors: Nobel Prizes in Chemistry, Physics and Medicine*. Minneapolis: Lerner, 1988. Written for middle school and junior high audiences, this book includes a chapter that focuses on the actual invention of the transistor.

Thomas, Shirley. *Men of Space*. Philadelphia: Chilton, 1960. This series of books detailing the people who contributed to space age technology includes a chapter on Shockley. Unlike most such accounts involving scientific discovery, it provides more biographical information than technical detail.

Those Inventive Americans. Washington: National Geographic Society, 1971. Provides an understanding of Schockley's importance. Very readable for young adults.

Wilson Greatbatch
& the Implantable Pacemaker

Wilson Greatbatch holding an implantable pacemaker.
(Courtesy of Greatbatch Gen-Aid Ltd.)

*N*one of the technological marvels of this or any century can equal the one that each of us was given at birth—the human body. Wondrous as it is, however, this intricate, self-sustaining creation comes with no guarantee that all parts will function reliably. Failure or malfunction of human organs is a common reminder of the fragile nature of life. Throughout most of history, such failure has meant death or disability.

In the 20th century, medical inventors have taken up the challenge of prolonging human life by building substitute parts to replace the faulty ones. The most spectacular of these inventions are the artificial organs such as hearts and livers.

But the expense and the precision required by these impressive examples of engineering have limited the number of people who have benefited from them. Meanwhile, a tiny device no more complicated than an electrical flasher has quietly changed the lives of millions of people. The implantable pacemaker, dreamed up by an assistant in an animal laboratory, has been named one of the most important electrical engineering feats of the century.

In an age when so many inventions involve the joint efforts of many individuals, backed by massive infusions of money, the implantable pacemaker was a throwback to the old days of Edison and Bell. The first pacemakers were created by the hand of Wilson Greatbatch, working largely by himself in his farmhouse laboratory.

Wilson was born to Walter and Charlotte Greatbatch on September 6, 1919, in Buffalo, New York. Wilson's father had been born in England but now worked as a small contractor building homes in the Buffalo area. Wilson attended public school in West Seneca, New York, a small community southeast of the city.

Wilson's fascination with the mysterious nature of electronics began at an early age. He found it stimulating to deal with electricity—something that you could not see but that could do all sorts of amazing things.

Greatbatch's curiosity led him to build his own short-wave radio receiver when he was a teenager. The thrill of turning on his own set one day and capturing voices speaking from across the ocean in London fueled his enthusiasm. Looking for someone with whom he could share his hobby, he joined the Sea Scout Radio Division.

One evening in 1937, he was playing with the radio at the Sea Scout Base when he heard frantic calls from some East Coast radio stations. New England was being battered by a hurricane, and these stations were trying to get emergency messages out. Greatbatch and other operators in the club stayed on the air for 26 hours, passing along the messages they heard. Their efforts earned them a special citation from the Red Cross. Sea Scouts provided Greatbatch with an important social group as well as an outlet for his hobby interest.

In 1939, Greatbatch joined the U.S. Naval Reserve. Because of his experience with communications, Greatbatch was trained as a radio operator and spent some time repairing electronic equipment. But when the United States was drawn into World War II, he flew combat missions in the Pacific as a rear gunner on dive bombers and torpedo bombers. A third of his squadron mates were killed in action.

At the war's end, Greatbatch returned to Buffalo where he married Eleanor, a woman whom he'd met through Sea Scouts some years earlier. When it came to choosing a career, Greatbatch originally had modest ambitions. Before the war he had enrolled at Buffalo State Teachers College with intentions of being an industrial arts teacher.

But Greatbatch decided to take advantage of the GI Bill offering free education. After working a year as a telephone repairman, he applied to the School of Engineering at Cornell University in Ithaca, New York. It took an inventor's genius to get him into the school. Because Cornell had no housing for non-resident students, his application was turned down. Greatbatch got around that by scraping together enough money to buy a small farm south of town and then reapplied as a resident student. He was accepted in 1946.

After five years of surviving the terrors of war, Greatbatch had grown to savor the enjoyment of gaining new knowledge. He worked hard at his studies, although he never achieved outstanding grades at Cornell. In fact, he liked to joke that his only outstanding credential as a student was having the most children of all his classmates. In order to support his wife and three children born while at Cornell, Greatbatch had to work a variety of jobs. One of these was at the Psychology Department Animal Behavior Farm in Varna, New York. Greatbatch was put in charge of rigging instruments on roughly 100 goats and sheep so that such data as heart rate and blood pressure could be monitored.

Greatbatch continued to work at this farm after gaining his undergraduate degree in 1950, and it was there that he first heard of complete heart block. During the summer of 1951, he ate his lunches with two surgeons from the Boston area who had come to the Varna farm to perform experimental brain surgery on goats. While eating their brown-bag lunches, they discussed a variety of medical subjects. One day, they brought up the subject of heart block.

People afflicted with heart block have little control over their heartbeat. It can zoom up to several hundred beats per minute and then suddenly trail off to almost nothing. This can result in severe chest pains, fainting spells, loss of memory and awareness, and death.

The problem in heart block lies in a section of the heart called the sinus node. The sinus node is the heart's "pacemaker." It generates a tiny electrochemical shock every second or so that stimulates the heart, causing it to contract, or beat.

In heart block, the nerve that sends this impulse cannot get through to the ventricle, the actual pumping section of the heart. Without its triggering signal, the ventricle does not contract.

The body has a backup pacemaking system. If the ventricle does not beat within a certain period of time, an auxiliary pacemaker located much lower in the heart will take over and supply a random impulse of its own. This system, however, is not infallible either. If it malfunctions, the victim has what is called Stokes-Adams syndrome, and the outlook is grim. The body cannot survive for more than five minutes without a heart beat. Even a 15-second lapse between heartbeats usually causes fainting.

When Greatbatch heard the description of heart block, he immediately thought of a way to fix it. From his work with animal instrumentation, he was well aware that a heart could be made to beat by applying an electrical jolt. All that was needed to take over the function of the sinus node was to rig up some kind of regular, electrical impulse to the heart. Unfortunately, the vacuum tubes and storage batteries needed to provide such an impulse were far too bulky to put into a chest cavity. Greatbatch dismissed the matter for the time being.

Unknown to him, Dr. Paul Zoll of Boston was in the process of experimenting with external pacemakers that operated on power from a wall socket. In the early 1950s doctors began attaching these pacemakers to the patients' chest. Dr. C. Walter Lellehei, an open-heart surgeon at the University of Minnesota, achieved more effective results by attaching the pacemaker's electric wires, or electrode, directly into the muscle of the heart.

At about the same time, the transistors invented by Shockley and his team became commercially available. Not only were they much smaller than vacuum tubes, but they required only a tiny amount of power in order to work. Small batteries would easily do the trick. Battery-powered pacemakers built with transistors were small enough to be carried around by the patient.

Although these pacemakers offered more freedom to heart block victims, they still did not allow normal activity. There was always an open wound through which the wires were attached to the heart. Patients had to be careful that this wasn't bumped, and they could not allow it to get wet.

When Greatbatch saw his first transistor in 1953, he was intrigued by the possibilities of the device. Back in Buffalo in the mid-1950s, working as an assistant professor at the University of Buffalo, he began using them in his laboratory equipment. One day in 1956 he was attempting to build an oscillator, a current-generating device, he needed for recording heart sounds. He reached into a box to pull out the type of resistor, a device for controlling electric current, that he needed for his instrument. But he misread the identifying colors and so accidentally put in a different type of resistor than he had planned. To his astonishment, the circuit began to "chirp," sending out an electric signal at a rate of about once a second. Greatbatch found that the transistor was using only a tiny amount of current while performing in this way. By sheer accident he had discovered how to provide low-power impulses to the heart.

Greatbatch tried to interest a number of heart specialists in his implantable pacemaker idea. But after two years of presenting his plan to various groups, he was unable to generate any support.

At that time, Greatbatch was a member of a group of electrical engineers who were interested in medical instruments. This group set up monthly meetings to present technical information to engineers and interested people in the medical profession. They also provided engineering expertise for doctors who were having technical problems with their equipment.

One of those who came to the engineers' group for advice was Dr. William Chardack, chief of surgery at the Veteran's Administration Hospital in Buffalo. Greatbatch was part of the team assigned to help Chardack with his problem. Although the engineers were unable to solve the problem, Greatbatch made an important contact. One of Chardack's assistants happened to be a high school classmate of Greatbatch. With the former classmate's cooperation, Greatbatch was able to approach Chardack with his implantable pacemaker idea.

Chardack listened to the proposal and then spoke the words that would change Greatbatch's life: "If you can do that, you can save ten thousand lives a year."

Greatbatch was a deeply religious person. His first question when considering any new project was not "will it make money" but "is this a good thing?" Chardack's prediction was all the encouragement Greatbatch needed. He went home to his laboratory located in a wood-heated barn in back of his house. There he put together his first pacemaker.

Three weeks later, he was back at Chardack's hospital to give a demonstration on a dog. The animal's heart was blocked off with stitches. Then the wires of his miniature device were attached to the heart. Immediately it began to beat. An astonished Chardack agreed to join Greatbatch in producing this revolutionary technology.

As it turned out, the building of a pacemaker device was the easy part. The real challenge was making one that could survive in a living body. At first Greatbatch supposed that the device could be sealed off from body fluids with electrical tape. His first pacemaker, however, survived only four hours inside a dog. Greatbatch quickly discovered that the interior of the human body is "a far more hostile environment than outer space or the bottom of the sea" because of the moisture, heat, body salts, and the need to avoid rejection by the body.

The effort to perfect the implantable pacemaker required knowledge in a number of scientific fields, and Greatbatch was grateful for the chemistry, physics, and math that Cornell had required of him. For the next two years he worked on ways of protecting the pacemaker without causing the body to reject it.

At that time he was working for Taber Instrument Corporation. Taber was not interested in pursuing his pacemaker because they were concerned about liability. They did not want to risk the huge lawsuits that might result if the device proved defective. As his pacemaker experiments began to take up more of his time, Greatbatch had to confront a risk of his own. Was he willing to risk his career on this invention of his? With enough savings in the bank to support his wife and, by this time, five children for two years, Greatbatch decided he could quit his job and devote all his time to the pacemaker.

More than most researchers, Greatbatch liked to work instinctively rather than follow an elaborate, step-by-step program. He later commented that if he did the same type of experimentation

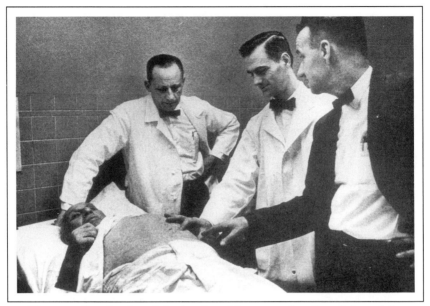

*The team that developed the implantable pacemaker: from left to right,
William Chardack, Andrew Gage, Wilson Greatbatch.*
(Courtesy of Veterans Administration Medical Center, Buffalo, New York)

under today's strict government regulation of medical research he would probably be sent to jail. Making a device in a barn and bringing it into a hospital without following rigid safety requirements would be strictly forbidden.

Rather than try to predict what might happen, Greatbatch preferred to go ahead with experiments. The results of one experiment would determine what he would try next. Greatbatch often came up with his best ideas in the late night and early morning hours when he could not sleep. Then he would rush down to the laboratory to try out the latest inspiration.

Eventually he found a way to encase the pacemaker in a solid block of epoxy, a hard thermosetting plastic. Later the devices were sealed in metal cases. After a year of experimentation in 1958–59, Greatbatch increased the survival time of the pacemaker in dogs from four hours to four months. Chardack and Gage offered their own suggestions for improving the device, and, in fact, the electrode used was designed by Chardack. Gradually, the pacemaker began to take shape. The original implantable pace-maker was a metal disk about 2½ inches in diameter and ⅝ of an inch thick. This provided an electric signal at one-second intervals. A pair of wires attached to the wall of the heart transferred this impulse to the heart.

Greatbatch spent all the money he had available, $2,000, hand-building about 50 of these pacemakers. The first 40 of these were implanted in dogs with steadily improving results. Although still far short of his goal of a five-year life for pacemakers, Greatbatch had made enough progress to turn his sights to human patients. A likely prospect turned up in 1960. A patient was suffering so terribly from heartblock that he had to wear a football helmet to protect himself from frequent falls caused by heart failure. He was not expected to live long.

In 1960, Chardack implanted a pacemaker in this patient and in nine others, including two children. The technique proved to be successful (the first pacemaker operated for 20 months) and Chardack published a paper describing his procedures that same year. He put his prestige on the line in advocating the use of this new technology to a sometimes skeptical medical profession.

The implantable pacemaker was not an overnight sensation. During the early operations about 10 percent of the patients, most of whom were high-risk cases, did not survive. For a number of years it remained a novelty operation, performed only rarely by a few physicians. But Chardack was able to convince his medical colleagues that the implantable pacemaker was an idea whose time had come.

News reports of the remarkable new technology centered on Chardack and his team and made no mention of the inventor. Greatbatch, however, had by no means disappeared from the scene. A small Minneapolis company called Medtronic, which had been making battery-operated external pacemakers, recognized the potential value of implantable pacemakers. In early 1961 they struck a licensing agreement with Greatbatch to manufacture his patented pacemaker. Greatbatch continued to build and test the pacemakers. His laboratory was still unsophisticated. He now had two ovens set up in his bedroom for sealing the pacemakers. Every transistor used was tested by Eleanor, who determined their ability to stand up to shock by tapping them with a pencil.

Greatbatch continued to modify and improve his pacemakers. They became smaller and more efficient. By 1965 he was able to develop a "demand" pacemaker. Instead of sending out an impulse every second whether it was needed or not, this device listened to the heart and provided an electric signal only when it was needed. New generation pacemakers were also designed so that the pace could be externally set and adjusted by a physician.

By 1970 virtually all of the flaws in the pacemaker had been perfected, and yet they continued to wear out after about two years. When Greatbatch determined that it was the battery that caused 80 percent of the failures, he insisted that they needed to focus their research on new batteries. Medtronic, however, recognized that such research might offend their battery suppliers. Rather than risk the possibility of losing their current supply of batteries, they declined Greatbatch's suggestion.

Greatbatch decided that the need for improved batteries was great enough for him to risk another career gamble. Although he knew nothing about making batteries, he sold his patents to Medtronic and went into battery manufacturing. Greatbatch looked into a number of novel approaches to the problem of short-lived batteries, including rechargeable and biological batteries, but he saw that they would not work. Nuclear-powered

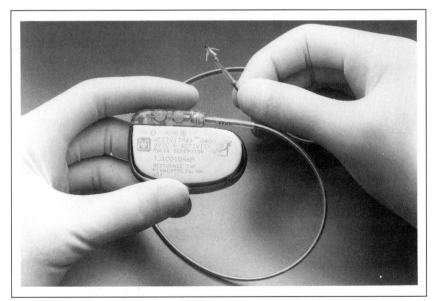

This titanium-cased pacemaker contains a sensor that adjusts the heart rate depending on the patient's activity level.
(Reprinted with permission of Medtronic, Inc. ©Medtronic, Inc., 1990)

batteries seemed to have greater possibilities. He spent two years trying to tailor plutonium 238 (a material now used in nuclear bombs) to use as a pacemaker battery. In the end he abandoned the idea as impractical.

Greatbatch finally discovered a lithium battery developed by Fred Teppen. As usual, he tinkered with these batteries until he came up with a reliable, injury-proof power source for pacemakers. These batteries were manufactured by his own company. The batteries have become the industry standard.

Once the technology for pacemakers was complete, Greatbatch moved into other areas of medical technology. Still working out of the Buffalo area in which he was raised, he has continually sought projects of benefit to humankind. Among the problems he has tackled are biomass energy conversion and plant genetics, and diseases such as leukemia and AIDS.

Throughout all of his years as a successful inventor, he has never forgotten the importance of the education that gave him his chance in the world of medical technology. The GI Bill made it possible for him to get the education that he could not have otherwise afforded. Greatbatch has decided to repay that favor many times over. One of the benefits his company offers is free tuition and books for all employees and their children.

During his career, Greatbatch has accumulated more than 150 patents. Of all his inventions, the implantable pacemaker has been by far the most significant. By the end of 1982, more than 650,000 people in the United States were walking around with artificial pacemakers triggering their heartbeats. By the end of the 1980s, pacemaker implants were being performed in the United States at the rate of 300,000 per year.

Currently, more than two million people in the United States are enjoying more complete lives because of Greatbatch's invention. Many of them have been supported by pacemakers for two decades. Prior to the pacemaker, the life expectancy of a person with Stokes-Adams complete heart block was about one year. Now the survival rate for such people is about the same as for the general population.

Unlike most of the other inventions in this book, the pacemaker was built for one specific purpose. Although pacemaker research solved problems that led to improvements in artificial organ technology, the pacemaker itself has not spawned a wealth of new products. Yet in 1983 the National Society of Professional Engineers selected the implantable pacemaker as one of the 10 most important engineering contributions of the past 50 years.

Greatbatch has had the rare privilege of seeing people without a future walk away from a hospital to live normal lives for decades, all because of his little 2-ounce device. As a grandfather he has learned to appreciate the fact that his invention has given hundreds of thousands of grandparents the opportunity to play with their grandchildren.

Chardack's prediction of saving 10,000 lives a year has proven to be far too modest. For each of those people given new life, the implantable pacemaker has been by far the most precious of all the 20th-century inventions.

Chronology

September 6, 1919	Wilson Greatbatch born in Buffalo, New York
1939	joins Naval Reserve
1945	returns to Buffalo after combat duty in Pacific
1946	enters School of Engineering at Cornell on GI Bill
1950	receives electrical engineering degree from Cornell
1951	learns of complete heart block while working at animal lab
1957	presents idea for implantable pacemaker to Dr. Chardack; begins experiments; is awarded master's degree from University of Buffalo
1960	Chardack's team implants first pacemaker; Greatbatch forms his first company, Wilson Greatbatch, Inc.
1965	Greatbatch develops demand pacemaker
1970–72	develops lithium battery for pacemaker
1985	Greatbatch incorporates a new research company, Greatbatch Gen-Aid, Ltd.

Further Reading

Brown, Kenneth A. *Inventors At Work*. Redmond, Washington: Microsoft Press, 1988. This book, which consists of interviews with 16 important American inventors, provides a rare personal view of this relatively unheralded inventor.

Gordon Gould & the Laser

Gordon Gould
(UPI/Bettmann)

As William Shockley once said, many modern inventions "are predicted in advance by science from fundamental knowledge." When a new scientific insight predicts one of these inventions, there can be a wild scramble among inventors to be the first to put the prediction into practice. Sometimes this experimental stampede causes such confusion that it is difficult to tell who is the first to do what.

This is exactly what happened with the origins of the laser. Locating the inventor of this marvelous device has been much like trying to solve a murder mystery. Over the years there have been enough conflicting evidence and false leads to point the finger of suspicion in a number of directions. It has been the unenviable

116

task of patent officials and federal judges to determine "whodunnit."

Was it the Bell Telephone Laboratories, as a number of scientists believed in the early 1960s? Or was it Theodore Maiman? On July 7, 1960, little more than a month before the Bell breakthrough, Maiman announced that he had built and tested a laser machine, the first operating model of a its kind. Did that make him the inventor, or did he just put together the pieces that had been invented by Charles Hard Townes? In the 1950s Townes, a 41-year-old Columbia University physics professor, had come up with a plan for building a microwave amplification device called a maser. In the late 1950s, he applied some of these concepts to visible light. Based on this work, Townes and his brother-in-law, Arthur Schawlow, were awarded the first patents pertaining to lasers. This work led to a Nobel Prize in physics for Townes and recognition as the inventor of the laser.

However, after more than 20 years of sifting through the evidence, patent experts ruled that there was someone with an even stronger claim as the inventor of the laser. Gordon Gould, a graduate student who was at Columbia University while Townes was teaching there, was finally declared the rightful creator of one of the most spectacular and versatile innovations in history.

Gordon Gould was born in New York City on July 17, 1920, the son of Kenneth Miller and Helen Gould. His mother, who raised him and whose last name he took, was a mechanically talented person, and she taught some of those gifts to her son. When Gordon was three years old, she bought a kind of construction kit called an Erector set. Recognizing that children of that age are often quicker to demolish than to build, she did the constructing and let Gordon take apart what she had made. Eventually, Gordon took over the constructing and his mom did the dismantling. As he was growing up Gordon developed a keen interest in working with his hands. He and his brothers were frequently building or fixing some device, such as clocks. By the time he reached high school, Gordon dreamed of making his living as an inventor.

His interest in discovering how things worked led him into the area of physics. Gould attended Union College in Schenectady, New York, and received a bachelor of science degree in physics in 1941. That summer he entered the job market and found work at

Western Electric. He quickly became disillusioned, though, when he noticed that all the important positions in the company were filled by much older men. Unwilling to spend many years climbing the corporate ladder, he quit his job and went back to school at Yale University.

It was there that he was introduced to the strange relationship between light and matter. For many years a battle had raged among physicists as to the basic nature of light. Was light made up of particles, like matter, or was it made up of waves, like sound? The famous physicist Albert Einstein shook up the world of physics in 1905 by arguing that light was made up of a form of energy called photons that could behave as both a particle and a wave.

Since that time, it had been determined that light could be caused by the movement of electrons in an atom. Electrons orbit the nucleus of the atom, and the farther their orbit is from the nucleus, the more energy they have. In some atoms these electrons can jump to a more distant, high-energy orbit after being exposed to an energy source. This is known as an excited state. Atoms do not stay in an excited state for long. When the electrons return to their original lower-energy orbit, they release the extra energy in the form of photons.

Gould studied a great deal about light while earning his master's degree at Yale. While he was finishing his studies, he was recruited by the United States government for its gigantic, secret effort to construct an atomic bomb. From 1943–45, Gould worked in the Manhattan Project labs in New York City. (Manhattan Project was the code name for this work.) Following the war, he taught at City College of New York.

During this time, Gould and his first wife became interested in the theories of Karl Marx, a German philosopher whose theories paved the way for Russia's communist revolution, and they joined a Marxist study group. After the 1948 Soviet takeover in Czechoslovakia, Gould lost his enthusiasm for Marxism. This dabbling in politics disrupted his whole life, and he got caught in the crossfire from both sides. His rejection of Marxism created a rift between him and his wife, and the two eventually divorced. But his brief involvement with the group later created serious problems for him with the United States government and severely hampered his efforts at building a laser.

Gould left his teaching position in 1954 and went to Columbia University to study for his doctorate degree. Columbia was the center of microwave research in the world and included among its faculty Charles Hard Townes, the inventor of the maser. *Maser* is an acronym for Microwave Amplification by Stimulated Emission of Radiation. It was basically a device for making microwaves—extremely short electromagnetic waves—more powerful.

While much of this microwave research was going on, Gould was studying both microwaves and the much longer light waves. Gould had never given up on the idea of being an inventor, and despite his many years of study in physics, he never considered himself a scientist. He was not interested in basic research as much as he was in inventing some new product—a product that would be of use to ordinary people as well as researchers.

Gould was well aware of the possibilities that existed for inventing something that could make use of the surprising power of light. He knew from Einstein's work that light could stimulate atoms into an excited state and cause them to absorb light energy. He also knew that Einstein had predicted back in 1917 that the reverse of this was true, that light could stimulate excited atoms into giving off light energy. The light energy released would be very powerful because it would be coherent light.

Coherent light simply means light that is all of one wavelength. The light from a lamp is incoherent light. It includes many different wavelenghts of light scattered in all directions and so its energy is quickly diluted. In coherent light all the energy is concentrated in only one wavelength so it is very powerful. If this coherent light could be focused in a single direction, the energy would be far more concentrated yet. Up to that time, however, no one had figured out how to stimulate light emission, much less amplify and focus it.

Gordon Gould pondered the problem while working at home on his doctoral thesis. He began to develop a plan for pumping light into a substance so that it would cause light emission. In October of 1957, he received a call from Charles Townes, asking him for information about high-energy lamps. That alerted Gould to the fact that there were other researchers who were working on light emissions also. He had to act fast if he was to be the first to make a discovery.

Gould was lying in his bed, unable to sleep late on the night of November 11, 1957, as he puzzled over the problem of optical pumping. Suddenly the answer came to him and, he saw how to build a laser. Since no one was clamoring for a machine that could emit powerful light, he was not certain what use this device would have, but he was convinced he had made an important discovery. This was a Saturday night, and he spent the rest of the weekend writing down his thoughts and sketching rough drawings into his notebook. On the first page of that book, he used a new term, based on Townes' "maser," to describe his invention. *Laser* stood for Light Amplification by Stimulated Emission of Radiation.

Gould then did some calculations to figure out how much energy could be produced by light amplification. The results were staggering. According to his figures, a laser could conceivably heat a substance to the temperature of the sun in a millionth of a second! When he saw what kind of power could be produced with a laser, Gould knew that he was on to something big. At the end of his notebook he listed a number of potential uses for a laser, including radar, communications, and heating.

In order to prevent someone from stealing his discovery, Gould dashed out on Monday to a nearby candy store, whose manager was a notary public, a person who is authorized to witness legal documents. Gould had his notebook notarized, an action that was crucial in later establishing his claim as the laser inventor.

Unfortunately, he received some bad legal advice. He was told that he could not patent his ideas unless he first could provide a working model incorporating them. Gould realized that the professor under whom he studied at Columbia favored pure research for the advancement of scientific knowledge, and would probably discourage him from working on a practical invention. Even though it meant abandoning his work on his Ph.D., Gould decided to quit school in 1958 so that he could work on the laser.

Gould knew that he needed both financial and technical help in order to produce a working laser, and so he joined a company called Technical Research Group, Incorporated (TRG), in Long Island, New York. TRG was a small company, employing 30 to 40 scientists, that put a premium on creativity.

The most difficult part of designing a laser was finding effective ways to stimulate or energize the selected atoms. Gould thought of half a dozen possible ways to do this. Two of these methods have become standard techniques in the laser industry.

One of these was the optical pump, in which a lamp is coiled around a tube of excitable solid material. Photons from the bright light of the lamp energize these atoms and cause their electrons to reach an excited state. When the electrons return to their normal state, the atom releases photons that are all of the same wavelength. These photons are reflected back and forth through the tube of material by a silver coating on the ends of the tube. Each time they pass through the tube, the photons excite more atoms, which release more photons, until the coherent light becomes very strong. At some point, the beam of photons becomes powerful enough to break through one of the silver mirrors and can be directed toward the target.

Gould's other method was the gas discharge laser, in which the excitable material is a combination of gases, such as neon and helium or carbon dioxide and nitrogen. An electric current is directed through a gas-filled tube, where the electrons collide with and excite the atoms of the gases so that they release photons.

While Gould was working out the details of his invention, Townes and his brother-in-law Schawlow, a physicist working for the Bell Telephone Laboratories, had also discovered the principles on which a laser could be built. They filed their first laser patents in 1958. Gould did not enter his first laser patent claims until the following year. By that time, it was too late. Although Gould's patent applications contained a good deal of information that was not included in the Townes-Schawlow application, there was enough overlap between the rivals so that Gould's was rejected.

Gould was dealt another devastating setback by the government's national security system. Having recognized the potential of the laser as a weapon, he developed a proposal for TRG to submit to the United States armed forces in 1959. TRG officials hoped that the military would provide them with $300,000 for laser research. Having learned a painful lesson from Robert Goddard about ignoring new avenues of technology, the military not only accepted the proposal but more than tripled its funding to a million dollars! But while the money was helpful, the government regulations that came with it were not. The project was classified as a government secret, which meant that only carefully screened people would have access to it. One of those who did not make it through the screening process was Gordon Gould. Because of his past association with a Marxist group, Gould was considered a bad security risk and was denied permission to work on the project. Even more frustrating, his own notebooks on the subject of lasers were classified as secret and so Gould could not even look at his own work!

With Gould barred from leading the project, TRG's laser project lagged. The honor of developing the first operating laser went to

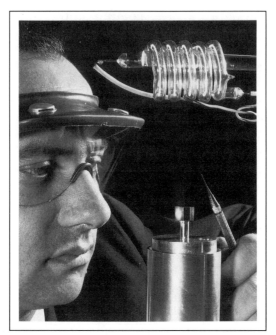

Theodore Maiman, who put together the first working laser, positions a synthetic ruby crystal. The light source at top excites the atoms of the ruby to produce amplified light.
(Courtesy of Hughes Research Laboratories)

Theodore Maiman of the Hughes Aircraft Company, in 1960. Maiman discovered that a ruby worked well as the excitable *lasing medium* at the heart of his laser.

Gould was not about to give up ownership of his invention without a fight. He filed appeals to the patent authorities to grant him the patents to which he felt entitled. Ironically, one of the reasons that the government denied his claims was that he had not met the requirement of "continuous work" on his idea. The only reason why he had not worked continuously on the project was because the government had not allowed him to! Gould began slipping into obscurity while others reaped the acclaim for the marvelous new laser.

The inventor carried his fight to the federal courts in what was becoming an increasingly complex legal battle. He was so confident of his final victory in the patent suits that he splurged and bought a large cruise boat. For six weeks each year, Gould would sail the Caribbean Sea in his boat.

But the court cases dragged on and on. Gould could not sit around and wait to collect his money. He continued to work for TRG, which merged into Control Data Corporation in 1965. Two years later he pulled out of this growing corporation for a chance to get back into research. Gould accepted a position as a professor at the Polytechnic Institute of New York, in Brooklyn. Feeling restricted by the school's limited research budget, he left in 1973 to form his own company, Optelecom, Inc. This venture specialized in optical communications.

As the laser industry began to flourish and laser patents became increasingly valuable, the stakes in outcome of the legal battles soared even higher. For Gould, there was more than personal pride at issue. In 1970 Control Data had pulled out of the laser business and had returned all of their patent rights to Gould. If he could establish just a few of his claims to laser technology, he stood to collect millions of dollars.

At first Gould was able to finance his legal appeals by selling a large amount of stock that had been given to him by TRG as a reward for landing the military contract back in 1959. But in the early 1970s, he was reaching the end of his financial resources. The only solution was to find someone who would pay his legal bills in exchange for some of the expected royalties.

Gould found enough investors to keep him going until he won his first court victory in 1973, nearly 16 years after he first thought of a way to energize a laser. That year a court ruled that there was not enough information in the original Townes-Schawlow laser patents to show how to build a laser. With this obstacle out of the way, Gould's patents had a chance.

It was not until four years later that Gould finally celebrated his first patent award. In October of 1977, Gould was given a patent for his optic pump.

But it turned out that he had exhausted his resources to get this far, only to discover new and more powerful opponents entering the fight. Giant corporations such as AT&T and General Motors had already paid out enormous licensing fees to other patent holders for the right to develop laser equipment. The prospect of now having to settle up with Gould for that same equipment sent their lawyers into action.

The new legal challenges were more than Gould could handle. He had already thrown $100,000 of his own money into the case. In 1979 he enlisted a company called Patlex to fight the legal wars in exchange for 64 percent of his royalties. Patlex spent more than $2.5 million on the Gould patents from 1981 to 1986 without getting a penny in return.

Finally in 1986 the United States Patent Office Appeals Board overruled all previous objections to Gould's patents. The following year Gould was also granted a patent for his gas-discharge laser, widely used in supermarket check-out scanners and hospitals. After more than 28 years of wrangling, Gould had finally won. The 67-year old man, two years into retirement, could rest and enjoy the long-awaited payoff from his invention.

During the early years of the marathon legal fight, the laser was considered an interesting but useless invention. By the time Gould's case was finished it was well-established as one of the most dynamic innovations in modern history.

By means of the laser, humans were able to harness incredible sources of power not previously available. Never before had humans been able to focus such incredible concentration of energy with such control. A laser can obliterate a tiny dot of material while leaving the area around it unharmed. This made it ideal for such delicate medical surgeries as killing cancer cells, removing birthmarks and kidney stones, clearing out clogged arteries, and correcting eye problems. The searing power of a laser could perform many jobs for heavy industry such as spot welding, drilling diamonds, cutting metal, and even repairing equipment sealed inside a casing. The laser has provided the only realistic hope of achieving the cheap, safe energy of nuclear fusion—the union of atomic nuclei resulting in the release of energy. The dream of using the laser as a weapon for wiping out incoming missiles has spurred the United States military to pour billions of dollars into laser research.

Lasers can do far more than focus heat. Because a coherent laser beam does not diffuse, or spread out, it can be used as a measuring device. Lasers can measure the distance to the moon with incredible accuracy, have been used in surveying, and have been used in quality control to ensure that machine parts are built to exact specifications.

Gordon Gould

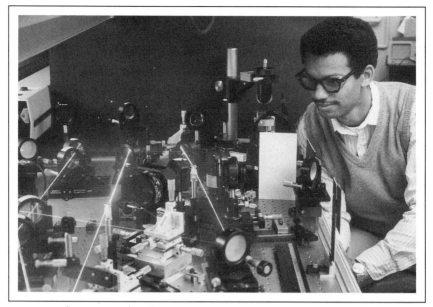

A Hughes Research Laboratories engineer adjusts a laser used in data processing.
(Courtesy of Hughes Research Laboratories)

Lasers have also proven ideal for use in communication. A single laser beam is able to carry thousands of signals at one time and so has vast potential for telephone and television systems. The laser's ability to relay and store information has made possible the universal product code that has greatly improved the efficiency of check-out counters in supermarkets and department stores. Lasers have already found their way into consumer homes in the form of compact discs that render an almost perfect reproduction of recorded sound.

Gordon Gould had the pleasure of experiencing one of the miracles made possible by his own invention. Without two eye operations performed with lasers, Gould would have lost his sight.

It cannot be said that Gould would have been blind if it had not been for that flash of inspiration in 1957, or that the hundreds of other changes introduced to society by the laser are owed to him. Too many people had been closing in on the laser for it to have escaped notice, with or without him. But the fact that others have since reached the South Pole and scaled Mt. Everest has not diminished the stature of those who reached these places first. Similarly, the fact that that Gordon Gould got to the laser first qualifies him as one of the influential inventors of the 20th century.

Chronology

―――――――

July 17, 1920	Gordon Gould born in New York City
1941	receives B.S. from Union College
1943	receives M.S. from Yale University
1943–45	works on U.S. government's atomic bomb project
1945	serves as a professor at City College of New York
1954	enrolls at Columbia University; Charles Hard Townes develops the maser
November 11, 1957	Gould discovers way to build a laser
1958	leaves Columbia to work on laser; joins Technical Research Group
1959	his laser proposal on behalf of Technical Research Group wins approval of U.S. government; Gould not allowed to participate
1967	Gould becomes professor at Polytechnic Institute in Brooklyn, New York
1973	forms Optelecom, Inc., Gaithersburg, Maryland
1977	obtains first patent for optical pump
1986	gains clear patent rights to major laser components

Further Reading

Brown, Kenneth A. *Inventors at Work*. Redmond, Washington: Microsoft Press, 1988. In this book, which also includes Wilson Greatbatch, the author picks Gould's brain. The result provides less biographical material than one might desire, but gives insight into the inventor's thoughts and personal philosophies.

Peltz, James F., "Bright Lights, Big Money," *Discovery*, March 1988. This article deals primarily with Gould's marathon legal battle to gain control of laser patents. It also includes a good explanation of the mechanics of the laser.

Index
Bold numbers indicate main headings

Index

Index

Index